ROYAL
ROLLS-ROYCE
MOTOR CARS

ROYAL
ROLLS-ROYCE
MOTOR CARS

ANDREW PASTOUNA

OSPREY
AUTOMOTIVE

HALF TITLE PAGE *The Queen visits the British Army of The Rhine as part of the Jubilee Review in 1977.*

TITLE PAGE *The first Rolls-Royce State car, the Queen's original Phantom IV, was designed from its inception to carry the unique radiator mascot of St George slaying the dragon. Whilst there was a mixed fleet of State cars in the Royal Mews, this mascot could be transferred to any of the remaining Daimlers.*

Page 8: The minutiae of international protocol, defined in memoranda between coachbuilder and Royal customer.

Published in 1991 by Osprey Publishing

59 Grosvenor Street, London W1X 9DA

© Copyright Andrew Pastouna 1991

British Library Cataloguing in Publication Data

Pastouna, Andrew
Royal Rolls-Royce motor cars.
1. Great Britain. Cars. History
I. Title
629.22220941

ISBN 1–85532–142–4

Editor Shaun Barrington
Designer Simon Bell

Filmset by Keyspools Limited, Golborne, Warrington
Printed in England

In appreciation for the help given by the Rolls-Royce Enthusiasts' Club in the preparation of this book, a percentage of royalties from its sale has been donated to the Sir Henry Royce Memorial Foundation.

CONTENTS

* In accordance with the Rolls-Royce practice of not using the number thirteen for any of its cars, there is no chapter 13 in this book.

ROYAL MEWS
BUCKINGHAM PALACE

TELEPHONE
WHITEHALL 4832

NOTE ON THE USE OF ROYAL EMBLEMS ON MOTOR CARS IN
COLONIAL TERRITORIES
_____

The Queen has approved that:

(a)   The Royal Arms with Supporters may be painted on
the door panels of the motor cars of Colonial Governors
General and Governors.   It is equally appropriate for
Governors General and Governors to have their own Arms
and monograms painted on the door panels.   The Royal
Cypher should not be used for this purpose.

(b)   The Royal Arms may only be worn on the Shield of
a motor car when The Queen is actually travelling in
it.   For a visit by Her Majesty such Shields should
be ordered through the Crown Equerry and must be returned to him at the end of the visit.

    It is customary for Colonial Governors and Governors,
as well as having a replica of their flag in miniature on the
radiator of their cars, to fly it on the bonnet.   A chromium
plated crown is also normally fitted to the front and rear
number plates in place of registration numbers.

13th November 1959

    Royce.

can be
ntre of the
ith Royal
that the two
lone on some
ew Zealand.
proximately

building in
f above the
ther an
ild be to
side lamps.

b) <u>Flagstaff Attachment</u> – H.M.The Queen does not
approve the flying of flags from the radiator cap of any
car in which she travels.   In the Directive issued by
Buckingham Palace on this subject it states that flags
should be flown from the front wing on open cars <u>only</u> and
from the roof of closed cars.

    The new internally illuminated shields used by the
Queen and the Queen Mother are provided with a tapped
socket for carrying a flagstaff.   The shields already held
by the Australian Commonwealth can easily have added a
tapped socket to carry a flagstaff, see also para 8d.   The
standard tapping for Royal flag sockets is ¼" B.S.F. and
this tapping suits the Edgington type flagstaff of which
the Australian Commonwealth have acquired a considerable
number.

    Would you please inform us when we design the flag
staff socket for the radiator cap whether it is intended
to have the flagstaff in addition to the Rolls-Royce
mascot, bearing in mind that the present standard arrangement of radiator cap does not permit easy removal of
say, the mascot and substitution by another cap carrying
a flag socket. (See also paras.8(d) and(e).

    c) <u>Arrangement for Shields Carrying Coats of Arms</u> –
It is noted that the Australian Commonwealth Dept. would
like the method for carrying shields on these cars to be
similar to that fitted to the Royal State cars here.

contd.

FOREWORD BY
HRH THE DUKE OF GLOUCESTER

There was a time when transporting the Monarch from one place to another involved many carriages and squadrons of cavalry to ensure that the inadequate roads were kept clear of blockages. The coming of the railways solved these problems for most journeys, but in the twentieth century the motor car has become for everybody the most practical expression of personal mobility.

This book explains how Rolls-Royce has provided Her Majesty with the kind of transport most suitable for official occasions. Formal events, where large numbers of people have assembled, require a precision beyond that of mundane motoring.

The very sound of the name Rolls-Royce seems to imply the adjective Royal. However, for half a century the British Monarch used Daimler cars, tall and wide, they provided excellent vision both inside and outside but were less than agile. This book demonstrates how Rolls-Royce came eventually to replace the official Daimlers, several years after younger members of the family had shown a preference for Rolls-Royce.

My father enjoyed driving his Phantoms and took every opportunity to supplant the chauffeur. Handling such a large projectile took a lot of skill and I remember following him in a smaller and more agile car that needed considerably less braking on the corners.

Each chapter reveals how the Royal Rolls-Royce motor developed over the years to maintain the best criteria for the design of the Official State Car. There should be no doubt which motor is carrying the centre of attention. No crowd should be confused as to who they have come to see, as is so often the case when a long row of standard saloon cars sweep past and it is difficult to distinguish the chief guest from the aides and police officers accompanying.

Status and prestige are difficult to define in words but they are recognisable in the form of these splendid motor carriages, built by hand from individual designs, as had been the practice of pre-war coach builders, who took a standard chassis and engine from Rolls-Royce, or Daimler, or many other manufacturers, and created the body work to suit the customer in either a unique design or one of a limited number.

Today we enjoy the benefit of very well developed motor cars that are produced in huge numbers to absorb the development costs. The Rolls-Royces described in this book are the last of the traditional system and are a survival of the craftsmanship of the panel beaters, carpenters, veneerers, polishers and upholsterers who created the magnificent carriages that preceded the motor car, and came to create the impressive hand-built motor cars of the first half of the 20th century. A tradition that Andrew Pastouna has brought up to date by his most detailed account of these unique Rolls-Royces.

THE ROLLS-ROYCE ENTHUSIASTS'
CLUB

THE ROLLS-ROYCE ENTHUSIASTS' CLUB was founded in 1957 when a yeoman farmer, Edward Harris, advertised in the *Oxford Mail* inviting owners of pre-war Rolls-Royce cars to get together. The primary aim was to create a self-help organization to make things easier for the owners of these old and rather specialized machines to keep them on the road, and to enjoy the company of fellow enthusiasts.

The idea caught on, and soon the exchange of technical information, a news sheet, and well attended rallies and social activities were sure signs that the Club was here to stay. From such humble origins the RREC has flourished mightily. There are now some 6,500 members from almost 60 countries.

To cater for local interests, there are now no less than 36 sections of the Club. Most are in Britain and Continental Europe, but others are located in such diverse places as Hong Kong, Northern Canada and the US. The common objectives of all members are the ownership, maintenance, restoration and usage of Rolls-Royce products from 1904 to the present day. (This does, of course, include all the Bentley cars made from 1933 onwards – all of which have been built by Rolls-Royce.)

It has been said that Rolls-Royce enthusiasts enjoy perhaps the most distinguished club headquarters in the world. This is within the Hunt House, in the attractive country village of Paulerspury, Northamptonshire. The Hunt House, an impressive Victorian structure, was originally built by Lord Grafton as the home of the Grafton Hunt. Valued at £1 million, it is now the property of the Sir Henry Royce Memorial Foundation, an educational charitable trust set up by the RREC in 1977. The

Foundation's aims follow those of Sir Henry Royce: above all, the pursuit of engineering excellence. The aim is taken seriously as is made evident by the Foundation's series of exhibitions, prizes and bursaries to give positive encouragement to young engineers.

Within the Hunt House complex are housed the individual build histories of over 100,000 cars, 30,000 photographs and 30,000 technical drawings – all with the Rolls-Royce Company's blessing, since the Foundation is the official custodian of such records up to and including the Silver Shadow. Owners of these cars can, for a nominal fee, have photocopies of their own car's history, which may in some cases run to more than 50 pages.

There is also in the complex a 100-seat, fully equipped lecture theatre; the Maurice Booth Memorial Library which contains copies of virtually every book ever published on Rolls-Royce and Bentley (from the earliest handbook, through workshop manuals to motoring novels); an extensive restoration and demonstration workshop with the world's best selection of Rolls-Royce specialist tools; dining facilities; technical classroom; an exhibition of photographs; and a display of unique Rolls-Royce memorabilia. The Club shop stocks an extremely extensive range of Rolls-Royce and Bentley material, including copies of virtually every Rolls-Royce and Bentley book presently in print – and for several of which the Club has the only remaining available copies.

The Hunt House, Paulerspury. Owned by The Sir Henry Royce Memorial Foundation, it is the splendid headquarters of the Rolls-Royce Enthusiasts' Club.

One very widely appreciated facet of Hunt House activities is the provision of technical seminars. These are mainly model-based, where specialist instructors make the intricacies of the maintenance and repair of cars from Silver Ghost to Silver Shadow seem easy. So far, well over 2,000 members have attended in excess of 200 seminars.

The Club publishes its award-winning magazine *The Bulletin* on a bi-monthly basis. It is filled with technical information, helpful hints, some social chat, historical articles and details of the many events constantly being organized by the Club. A companion publication is *The Advertiser*, published every month. This contains details of cars and parts for sale, market trends, wants and services offered.

Annually, the Club organizes its prestigious Rally and Concours. This never fails to attract a huge entry; in recent years, over 1,000 Rolls-Royce and Bentley cars have been present – the largest such gathering in the world.

Other Club activities include tours at home and abroad, rallies, charity fund raising, technical teach-ins, advice to members, driving tests and a great variety of social events. These all help to promote the good fellowship that is a hallmark of the RREC.

One further aspect of Club activity is publishing books of particular interest and importance to the marque. Recent examples include: *Rolls-Royce and Bentley Experimental Cars* by Ian W. Rimmer, *Steel Chariots in the Desert* by S. C. Rolls, and *Pinnacle* (annually) edited by Malcolm Tucker.

This volume by Andrew Pastouna, is the first – of what it is hoped will be many – produced in association with Osprey Publishing. It has been made possible only by the untiring co-operation and assistance of their Managing Editor, Nicholas Collins, to whom the Club is greatly indebted.

ROY BROOKS *Chairman Publishing Sub-Committee RREC*

For further information regarding the RREC, please contact:

The Chief Executive, Rolls-Royce Enthusiasts' Club
The Hunt House, Paulerspury, Northamptonshire, NN12 7NA

INTRODUCTION

WHENEVER HER MAJESTY QUEEN ELIZABETH II OR other members of the Royal family travel on official engagements, then almost certainly at least part of the journey will include the use of a Rolls-Royce motor car. This holds true even if the trip involves considerable distances using other forms of transport. Often, one or more of the State fleet of cars will be sent ahead to be available at the destination. When visits abroad involve the use of the Royal Yacht *Britannia*, a Rolls-Royce can travel on board in its own specially constructed garage.

It may seem to most people quite natural that the British Monarchy should, for official transport, use the only make of motor car that can lay just claim to the sobriquet 'the best car in the world'. However, this has not always been the case. Queen Victoria was never known to travel in any type of motor car, (though she died before Henry Royce made his very first car in 1904).

It was Queen Victoria's son the Prince of Wales (later Edward VII) who became the first member of the Royal family to ride in a motor car. This was in a Daimler belonging to the motoring pioneer the first Lord Montague. In the closing year of the 19th century the Prince ordered his first car. Not unnaturally, it was a Daimler, the 6-horsepower, 2-cylinder model, with coachwork by Hooper. The Prince quickly became an enthusiast for this new form of locomotion. By the time of his coronation in 1902, he had no less than four motor cars – all Daimlers.

By the time of the death of HM Edward VII in 1910 and Coronation of George V, only the great State occasions were bringing the horse-drawn carriages onto the streets. Within a year, every member of the Royal family had the use of motor cars, with Daimlers predominating. The Daimler Company of Coventry continued to provide cars for the Sovereign until well into the reign of the present Queen. However, following her accession in 1952, there came a gradual move from the products of Coventry to those of Crewe.

As this book relates, in 1955, after three years of satisfactory service by Rolls-Royce cars on official duties, and in the wake of much discreet manoeuvring, the Company was finally granted the right to display the Royal Coat of Arms together with the words 'By appointment to Her Majesty Queen Elizabeth II motor car manufacturers'. Within five years Rolls-Royce were supreme in the field, having successfully challenged Daimler's 60-year lead as Royal Warrant holders. And the Crewe Company continue to hold that honour to this day.

Interestingly enough, since the time of the Silver Ghost Rolls-Royce had supplied cars to numerous members of the Royal family other than the Sovereign. For example, the Prince of Wales (later Edward VIII) took delivery of his first Rolls-Royce, a Barker limousine, in 1919; he was a great enthusiast for the marque and owned no less than ten examples including 20 hp, Phantom I and Phantom II.

Other Royal owners include the Queen Mother and Princess Margaret, who has owned more Rolls-Royce cars than any other member of today's Royal family, and made certain that very positive ideas of her own were included in their specification. His Royal Highness the Duke of Edinburgh is also known to have exerted strong influence regarding the selection and specification of Royal cars.

HRH the Prince Henry Duke of Gloucester, HRH Princess Marina Duchess of Kent, HRH Prince Michael of Kent and HRH the Princess Alexandra of Kent all owned and used Rolls-Royce cars on official duties. Some of those cars have covered prodigious mileages and there are interesting stories connected with each one. Naturally, there are some features that are not normally made public. For example, who would expect one of the Queen's cars to be called 'Oil Barrel', or one belonging to Princess Margaret to be known as 'Baron Montaigne'? Who had a Rolls-Royce quietly replaced because it did not come up to scratch, and which car is the favourite of Prince Charles?

The book also contains fascinating detail regarding the host of individual idiosyncrasies and varied requirements of Royal owners. These range from a fire extinguisher mounted on the front of the car to a 'detective's step', concealed lighting, high-lift seats to give onlookers a better view and special measures to ensure the privacy of the occupants. Such unusual features say much about the car's owner; and at times sorely taxed the skills of the coachbuilder.

The text and illustrations are the outcome of many years of dedicated research by the author who has long had in intense interest in this fascinating topic. He has also possessed several cars previously in Royal ownership, and has had the distinction of loaning his cars for use by various members of the Royal family on numerous occasions.

The book is intended for everyone interested in the British Monarchy; at the same time, with its factual detail of chassis numbers, coachbuilding and other specifications it has especial appeal for those who share an enthusiasm for Rolls-Royce; or, indeed, for the subject of automotive refinement and craftsmanship as a first principle.

ACKNOWLEDGEMENTS

IN BOOKS OF THIS NATURE, the compiler can only succeed through the kindness and cooperation of those who hold information on the subject, in this case principally The Royal Family and Rolls-Royce Motor Cars Ltd.

I am indebted for an enormous amount of help received from members of Her Majesty's Household: particularly the Crown Equerry, Lt Col. Sir John Miller M C, whose quarter-century economic stewardship of the Royal Mews has enabled that department to rise to the demands of the 20th century without losing its dignity or compromising its efficiency. I would like to thank him for answering my multitude of questions and allowing me access to those under his command who have given their help in the project.

I would like to thank the recently retired Mews Superintendant Major W. S. Phelps C V O, M B E who made chauffeurs available to talk to me and to check details, as well as allowing closer inspection of the cars of State than one normally enjoys.

Her Majesty Queen Elizabeth the Queen Mother's Household were very generous with their time, through Her Majesty's Comptroller Captain Sir Alastair Aird, similarly H R H the Princess Margaret Countess of Snowdon, through her Private Secretary the Lord Napier & Ettrick.

H R H the Duke of Gloucester kindly set time aside to talk about those cars built for his father and to supply photographs to illustrate them. His Private Secretary Lt Col. Sir Simon Bland was most helpful in tracing the occasional vehicle and for putting me in touch with the late Mr W. Prater who, after so many years as chauffeur to the Dukes of Gloucester, lived on their estate in Northampton.

H R H the Duke of Kent also assisted with photographs and material through his private secretary Lt Comdr Sir Richard Buckley. H R H Prince Michael of Kent through his Secretary, initially Miss Alison Dixon and latterly Miss V. J. Freeman, allowed access to information and new photographs to be taken of the most recent Phantom V I to be delivered to junior members of the Royal family.

H R H the Princess Alexandra of Kent's private secretary Miss Mona Mitchell was always most helpful in responding to my enquiries.

The Hon Gerald Lascelles kindly provided information about his mother the late Princess Royal; and His Grace the Duke of Fife's Principal Private Secetary Mrs Angela M. McAlpine also kindly supplied information on Princess Louise the Princess Royal.

I am also most thankful to two people on the Press Relations staff of Buckingham Palace who were so helpful in the initial stages of this book's preparation: Dame Anne Wall, Assistant Press Secretary to Her Majesty, and her successor Mr John Haslam.

Without the cooperation of Rolls-Royce Motor Cars Ltd there would simply be no book. My first contact with the Company was through David Preston, who is acknowledged to be the most helpful and approachable of people in the public relations industry. Although under great pressure from many other enquirers, he has always made himself available to answer the most involved of queries. I was also greatly helped by Dennis Miller-Williams one-time Public Relations Manager at Rolls-Royce. His opening of the Company's picture archives was an adventure in itself, both at Conduit Street and at Crewe.

Possibly the two men at Rolls-Royce with the most practical experience of dealing with Buckingham Palace are Roger Cra'ster and John Rowe. Roger Cra'ster was for a number of years the official contact between the Royal Mews and the Company. It speaks volumes that this relationship has run so smoothly for so long. John Rowe was the Customer Relations Manager at Conduit Street for many years. Previously he was very closely connected with ensuring the absolute reliability of the Rolls-Royce cars during his time at the service station in Hythe Road. He also accompanied the vehicles on their occasional forays overseas as the company's travelling representative.

At Conduit Street, at Hythe Road where Phantom V Is are still built, and at Crewe, a great many people have given of their time. In particular at Crewe Ian Rimmer and Roy Penlington were most helpful, Ian convincing the photographic department that I could be depended on to replace photographic prints in correct order, and Roy that I would return intact one of the very few 'Royal' Phantom V I handbooks. At Hythe Road, Peter Hand the Car Sales Coordinator allowed me onto the shop floor to view the painstaking construction of a very rare Phantom V I Landaulette.

Much valuable information has been culled from the extensive archives of the Rolls-Royce Enthusiasts' Club who are the official custodians of so very many of the Company's own historical records. General Secretary Lt Col. Eric Barras OBE and Chief Executive Peter Baines have given unstintingly of their time and expertise, along with Bunny Austin.

Very many other people have been most generous with their assistance. To them all, I am deeply grateful. They include: Sir Hector Monro; George Moseley and Arthur Johnstone (H. J. Mulliner); The late Osmond Rivers, Chief Designer, who wrote innumerable letters putting me right on so many points, Tom Smith and Colin Hyams, (Hoopers); David J. Smith, (Jack Barclay's); Peter Brockes, (N M M Reference Library); Paul Goodman, (Science Musuem, London); Eleanor M. Gehres, (Denver Public Library); Cpl Steve Baldwin R E of HQ 1st (Br) Corps (who so skilfully redrew the pre-war Duke of Kent's Wraith Landaulette line drawing); Philip Moss; Captain R. S. Clark R E; Flt Sgt S. R. Armstrong, R A F Lyneham; Steve Pavey, Ripon Barracks LAD; Robert Haswell (traced courtesy of the N U J); Colin Hughes; Jack Alpe; David M. King, New York; Ozzie Lyons, Norristown; Horton Schoellkopf, Silver Spring; Thomas E. Oliver, Mechanicsburg; Clyde Wade, Harrah's Automobile Collection, Reno; Tim Clarke, the Philippines; G. C. Francis M V O, who has over four reigns applied his skills as a Heraldic artist to many of the cars discussed in the book; Director J. M. Giles of Winterbotham, Strachan and Playne, Stroud; Alison Gamblin of Connolly Bros (Curriers); staff at Appleyard Rippon in Leeds who advised as to mechanical details, including Rolls-Royce Salesman John Thurland, and Geoff Ingle; and Klaus Rossfeldt. Thanks also to photographers Warren Allport and Jon Whitbourne.

Finally, I have to convey my gratitude to three tireless secretaries who kept cave whilst I worked during broadcasting hours, Jenny Moreland (now in Madrid), Alexandra Boscawen (in London) and Josephine Arengo-Jones (now in Berlin). Curiously, in the first and latter cases they went on to become extremely proficient broadcasters; maybe they were filling in for me at the time; or carving themselves new careers . . .

At the opening of the Mersey Tunnel in 1934, King George V and Queen Mary used one of their 1931 'Double Six' Daimler 40-50s. This is the Birkenhead end of the Tunnel.

1

THE STATE MOTOR CAR

MAJESTY IS ENHANCED BY A REGAL CARRIAGE. Since it is plainly impractical to surround the Monarch on the move with all the trappings and panoply of kingship, efforts have constantly been made to impress the multitude with fine horses and carriages, imposing trains, elegant yachts and – from the early part of this century – powerful and tasteful motor cars. It is with such cars and their Royal owners that this book is concerned.

It is to Edward VII – the first British monarch to ride in a motor car – that credit must go for the choice of colour that today adorns the State cars. His 1902 Daimler had its Hooper body painted in Royal Claret, a colour that out of the sunlight looks almost black. A few years later, King Edward added black mouldings to pick out the bodywork and a vermilion coachline to add distinction. His principal cars had the Royal Arms encircled by the collar of the Order of the Garter.

Although the general public had to register their cars from 1904, the cars in the King's ownership were exempted. It was in this year that the King decided to use his Daimlers for official duties as well as private engagements. During the reign of his son, George V, on the directive of the Minister of Transport, it was decided to license those vehicles of a more private nature, and since then only the State cars have escaped being registered.

Edward VII died in May 1910 having introduced motoring to the Royal Family and popularized it among the nobility. George V continued his father's lead in the use of motor transport. He added to the cars a number

LEFT *A closer look at the Daimler used to transport King George and Queen Mary at the Mersey Tunnel opening on March 18, 1934. The height of the Hooper coachwork can be gauged from this photograph. The mascot from this car is now on the Queen Mother's Rolls-Royce landaulette.*

BELOW *Another of the four post-war Daimler landaulettes carrying Queen Elizabeth (now the Queen Mother) along with a Lady in Waiting, her detective and chauffeur. As a State car it carried no registration plates.*

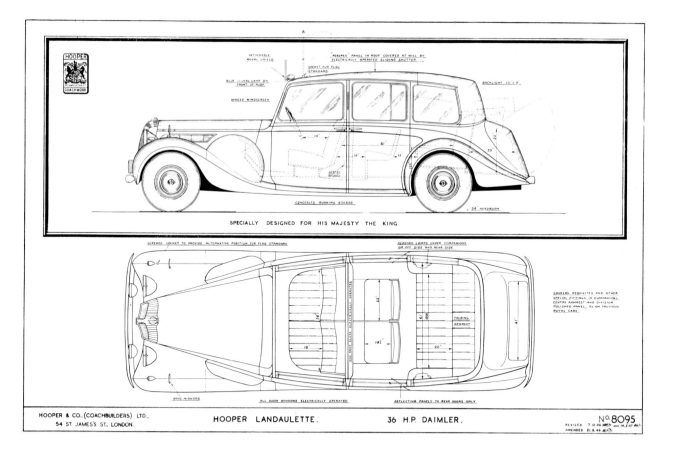

SPECIALLY DESIGNED FOR HIS MAJESTY THE KING

| HOOPER & CO.,(COACHBUILDERS) LTD., 54 ST. JAMES'S ST., LONDON. | HOOPER LANDAULETTE. | 36 H.P. DAIMLER. | N° 8095 |

ABOVE AND RIGHT
This car may look very much like a Rolls-Royce, but is in fact a 1940s Daimler that remained in Royal ownership until 1960. Here Prince Philip accompanied by the Royal children visits the Highland Games. It was the only landaulette to be converted to automatic head (hood) operation, in 1956. In 1989 it was purchased from Australia by Jaguar Cars, who now own Daimler.

of embellishments of his own in the next quarter of a century. Shields and flags became a prominent feature of the Daimlers when the King or Queen were about their business, the first of these appearing in 1911. After the First World War there were a great many more cars on the roads of Britain and to ensure priority for the Royal car at night, when the heraldic decorations could not be seen, a small blue light was fitted either above or below the windscreen; the position of the light seems to have been at the whim of the designer.

At the start of George V's reign most long journeys were still accomplished using the Royal train, but in the postwar period there was a great deal of industrial unrest and the railways were affected. Indeed, on one occasion the King was in Balmoral when he was required to be in London at short notice. In 1919 a journey of some 550 miles – even in a Royal Daimler limousine – was quite some feat; however, the run was split into two halves and the King arrived safely in the capital the day after his departure from his Scottish holiday home and was quite able to deal with his duties on arrival.

George V understood that the people wanted to see their monarch, and he and his wife, Queen Mary, always sat amidships on special centrally-placed chairs where a good view of them was afforded by the large main door windows. The King and Queen were always associated with high and massive Daimlers; the internal headroom on the earlier cars was a clear five feet.

At the time of King George V's Jubilee, in 1935, the internal height of his new 12-cylinder $6\frac{1}{2}$-litre Daimler had been reduced by a mere 3 inches. He and Queen Mary ordered a pair of these cars and they survived long enough to put in an appearance at the wedding of HRH Princess Elizabeth to Prince Philip of Greece in November 1947.

On the death of George V in January 1936, Edward VIII ascended the throne. During the short period of his reign – less than a year – King Edward introduced only one new idea into the operation of the Royal cars and this concerned the rear compartment illumination. By throwing a switch, the chauffeur could activate the three roof lamps in the rear of the car and he had control, too, over the step lights in the well of the rear doors. Although electric lighting had been on all Royal cars since 1904, the illumination had been intended for personal use. Until the advent of strip lighting in the 1950s as many as six rear compartment lights were used to illuminate the back of the car, all switched on by the chauffeur.

George VI, who was crowned in 1937, introduced a novel feature that has survived to the present day – the transparent roof to the rear compartment. This, coupled with his fondness for the landaulette style of coachwork (seven in all were constructed for his private and public use), enabled his people to enjoy a good view of him and his family. Although heaters had been introduced to luxury cars as far back as the early 1930s it was only during the Second World War that they were fitted retrospectively to the King's Daimler fleet.

However, when George VI came to order his first postwar Daimlers they fairly bristled with innovations. The 1947 Daimler State landaulettes had power operation to the windows, division glass and a blind which could cover the transparent section of the roof. Queen Mary was impressed enough to summon the Daimler Main Agents, Stratstone Ltd, and the liaison man with the Royal Family, Mr R. W. Cracknell, to Marlborough House. Here, the Stratstone man, who had just completed delivery to the elderly Queen of her new 27 hp Daimler, had to explain to Her Majesty that power operation of the division, which was a sideways winding division split vertically in the centre, could not now be provided. However, HM had primed one of her chauffeurs to make private enquiries at Hooper, who had built the body. Meanwhile, an agitated Mr Cracknell was quickly passing a note around the coachbuilders that should anyone inquire about power operation on Queen Mary's new car, then it could definitely not be done. So Her Majesty had to be content with the arrangement already fitted to her new green Daimler.

All the London coachbuilders patronized the same firm for electric winding motors, George Piper & Son. This firm had an edge on their competitors in that in the event of a failure a handle could be inserted at the bottom of the door and the window could be wound up manually, though it took a couple of dozen turns to accomplish it. When Rolls-Royce produced their own electric window lifts in the late 1950s demand for the Piper product shrank away. Hooper had many problems with power operation

Her Majesty the Queen Mother retained this Daimler landaulette on her fleet for some considerable time. It is seen here during a visit to Liverpool. The following car is the Earl of Derby's Silver Dawn (chassis S T H 99).

and a note on one Royal car file remarks: '. . . I feel that the present method (of getting cables to the motor) is not a workmanlike job and not one that we can afford to continue to fit to Hooper bodies'.

The problem was eventually solved by laying the cables for the power supply to the window motors in flexible conduits, but not before some embarrassing incidents: on one occasion The Queen Mother had to abandon her Daimler when the door frame supporting the motor caught fire. Another car eventually conveying Her Majesty to her destination.

The problems were not helped by the switching arrangement for the operation of the electric window lift, a two-button affair, one for up; one for down. By the late 1940s the electrical firm of Arrow Ltd, based in Plymouth, had perfected a reversible switch which required only pressure up or down on the rocker-switch to send the window in the direction required. Basically, the system remained unchanged until the new Phantom VI was delivered to The Queen in 1978; the windows in this case were fitted with permanent magnet motors, which provided, for the first time, fully adequate overload protection. Previous systems could inconveniently burn out at the motor instead of at the fuse.

Radio sets were fitted into George VI's State cars retrospectively in 1950. It seems that the King was reluctant to have a radio in the car in case onlookers might be under the impression that the occupants were more interested in the radio programme than in the place through which they were driving. The sets were installed in the cars as unobtrusively as possible, the control panel being in the rear centre armrest, where a cloth-covered lid enclosed the unit. The amplifier was in the boot, the speakers were behind the trim either side of the division, and the aerial was fitted under the floor. This latter position caused one or two problems as the aerial was apt to pick up snow, especially in the Highlands; and on one occasion the antenna was completely torn away.

The Daimler people had quite a lot of trouble installing the first wireless sets and Hooper, who were doing the installation along with Plessey, had to call in an electrician from Rolls-Royce to sort out a very persistent screening problem. The engineer went to the Western Avenue works of the coachbuilders, but was told in no uncertain terms by Rolls-

Royce that he was not to touch the Daimler Straight Eight engine. Nonetheless, his mission was a success.

There was much competition between the two major radio suppliers, Plessey and Radiomobile, and many a chauffeur was encouraged to go for this or that type of set. Plessey were in all the Royal Daimlers and Radiomobile in the Rolls-Royces subsequently supplied to the Palace; apart from that put into the Phantom V State landaulette built for the Queen Mother. Her Majesty remained faithful to Plessey. At first, they were all seven-valve affairs with especially selected long-lasting valves, but the 1960 and 1961 Phantom Vs were fitted with hybrid receivers with part valve and part transistor operation. However, the earlier Phantom IVs have since been converted to more modern appliances, whilst the two latest Phantom VIs have a cassette player as well as radio receiver.

Nowadays, the radios are maintained by Bicester Car Radio, whose owner, Royston Harris, has worked on the Royal cars since 1951, at which time he was in the employ of Radiomobile. His company also looks after the set installed in the Queen Mother's Daimler as well as her Phantom V.

Today, as in the reign of Edward VII over 80 years ago, the State cars carry the livery of Royal Claret and Royal Black – there are, surprisingly, 13 shades of black – plus, the vermilion coachline. For many years now the company providing the paint for the Royal cars, first Daimler and later Rolls-Royce, has been Thornley & Knight. They are still in Birmingham, and the paint is mixed on the same site as it was eight decades ago, at Bordesley Green Road. However, they operate today within the company who now own them, Croda Paints. They also make the special matt black for the Duke of Gloucester's car. Should you wish to repaint your own car in the Royal scheme you will be told that the colour is a special matching for the Royal cars only and the company is not allowed to supply either Royal Claret or Royal Black synthetic enamel paint other than to approved trade outlets for use on the Royal cars.

2

INTER-WAR YEARS

THE ROLLS-ROYCE cars built for members of the Royal Family between the two World Wars were designed primarily for private use. Most Royal owners kept Daimlers for their public engagements. It was the efficient operation of Rolls-Royce cars that undoubtedly paved the way for the ascendancy of that company over Daimler after 1945, but it was apparent from as early as the 1930s, and especially the latter part of that decade, that Rolls-Royce were very gradually edging their way into the Royal Family's public life.

There is no record of any member of the Royal Family owning a Rolls-Royce prior to 1919, although of course many travelled in them from time to time. The earliest mentions are a drive by the Duke of Connaught (one of Queen Victoria's sons) in a 10 hp when the Hon Charles Rolls accompanied Prince Arthur on a short demonstration in late 1904. The car may have been a Royce, manufactured prior to the new titling agreement. The nearest the company came to stealing a march on Daimler was in the supply of eight cars to the Government of India for the Delhi Durbar and tour of India in 1912 by King George V and Queen Mary.

But it was probably the First World War that introduced many members of the Royal Family to Rolls-Royces. The King used them on several of his visits to the British Expeditionary Force in France. The Prince of Wales also used them occasionally although he had his own Barker-bodied Daimler with him in France towards Christmas 1914.

One well-known story concerns a day in September 1917 when the Prince left his Rolls-Royce staff car and walked a few hundred yards to inspect some establishment. He was halted by an almighty explosion. Quickly retracing his steps, he discovered his chauffeur slumped dead over the wheel of the car, killed by shrapnel. It is then said that the Prince had the coachwork removed and sent back to the United Kingdom for mounting on a new chassis. However, this seems unlikely because such orders were no longer being executed at the works. Nevertheless, the story does go on to tell that a new chassis was built from spare parts to fulfil the Royal request.

Reading through the Rolls-Royce chassis cards for this period reveals that about 200 chassis were completed in the period 1915–17. It is doubtful if any of them could have been for anything other than armoured cars, staff cars and the like.

There is a mystery, though, which surrounds chassis 30 PD, ordered on November 19, 1915 for the Czar of Russia. This was an Alpine-type chassis and it was ready for dispatch to Barkers coachbuilders in January 1917, which seems an inordinately long time for a chassis to be in construction. At the time of the tester's approval of the chassis the name of the purchaser was crossed through and 'Prince of Wales' written in. But later in the records there appears the endorsement 'Car used by military on home or active service, European War 1914–19'. This particular car, however, was recorded in April 1919 as being back at Rolls-Royce for repair and later disposal to a buyer living in Finsbury Square, London.

It seems in retrospect that the Prince of Wales was unable to take delivery of the car; his war effort at that time would certainly have made it very difficult because of his travelling around the operations area. In the spring of 1916 he was in the Middle East, then he was on the staff of the XIV Army Corps in France and was involved in the Battle at Passchendaele before being posted in the autumn of 1917 to Italy, where he stayed until May 1918. After that the Prince returned to France and was attached to the Canadian Corps where he remained until the Armistice.

If the Prince was going to have a Rolls-Royce, it is probable that the company would have decided that he should have the latest model. What is certain is that in October 1919 an order from the Prince was received for a new chassis; it was allocated the number 31 PP, and it was dispatched to Barkers for an enclosed-driver cabriolet body to be fitted. Chassis 31 PP was

Queen Victoria's second youngest son, H R H Prince Arthur
The Duke of Connaught with the Honourable Charles Rolls in
a very early Royce-built 10 H P car.

the first postwar sanction and embraced a number of improvements including a starter motor built by the company. It was also fitted with aluminium pistons, which enabled the car to achieve 78 mph with a fully-equipped touring body.

At the same time as chassis 31 P P was going through the works, the Prince was allocated another chassis, this one numbered 9 L W. Both Silver Ghosts were bodied by Barker, but unlike 31 P P his second car was ordered with closed bodywork.

Both Silver Ghosts were delivered to the Prince on the same day, November 18, 1920. Whereas the closed car was with the Prince for four years, 31 P P was sold after only two years. Most interestingly, this was the car that was purchased by Miss Edwina Ashley as a wedding present for her husband, Lord Mountbatten. When he sold his wedding present two years later he bought another Rolls-Royce and stayed faithful to the marque for many years to come. The Prince's second 1920 Silver Ghost was eventually sold in June 1924 to an Ascot man, by which time the Prince had purchased two of the new 20 hp models.

Many Rolls-Royce cars were acquired for use as staff cars during World War I. HM The King and The Prince of Wales have disembarked from a Silver Ghost staff car to examine a gas bomb near the front line trenches in France, 1917.

A mystery surrounds two other Silver Ghosts which are supposed to have been owned by the Prince. Chassis 127 LW was destined for use in Switzerland and appears to have been delivered to the order of W. A. Schmidt with an all-weather body and all the necessary requirements for the Swiss climate, including a louvred bonnet. The car left Boulogne having crossed from Dover on June 24, 1925, but later service records show that the Prince of Wales had possession of the car from November 1929. The other Silver Ghost, chassis 1346 was a much earlier production, dating from 1910, and substantial claims have been made for its Royal ownership. The original owner was Major J. J. Richardson of the 13th Hussars, residing in Aldershot; later in its life the car was owned by G. Campling, of Piccadilly, London. But by November 1929 it, too, seems to have gravitated to the Prince of Wales. This last car was by then sporting a body not unlike the shooting brakes supplied by Hooper to the King, using Daimler chassis. They were for use on the estates during the game season. We can conjecture that both chassis may well have been stripped of their original bodies and new ones mounted. The cars would then have been used either at Balmoral or at Sandringham. In the case of chassis 1346, Balmoral is more likely because its subsequent owner was Sir Hector Mackenzie of Gairlock, about 120 miles from the Royal estate. Nowadays this car, still sporting its shooting brake body, is in the United States.

If the Prince had been appreciative of the Silver Ghost, he was, if anything, more enthusiastic about its smaller counterpart, the 20 hp. He purchased three of this model within four years and all were fitted with Barker bodies. The first was chassis 57 S 6 and it was delivered in August 1923 as an enclosed cabriolet. His second chassis, GA 14, with a two-seater cabriolet design, was delivered in December 1923. His final 20 hp came in December 1926 and was chassis GYK 49. By now the little 20 hp was fitted with four-wheel brakes and the Prince instructed Barkers to fit a sedanca limousine body. Eventually, when he disposed of the car, it was acquired by the Prince's one-time close friend and society hostess, Lady Emerald Cunard. She purchased it in March 1931.

Despite the 20 hp being the company's junior chassis, it was with this model that quite a few members of the Royal Family first became Rolls-

Royce owners. There is some dispute about Princess Mary, King George V's only daughter, having purchased a Rolls-Royce Silver Ghost. She had been given a secondhand Daimler by her father in 1920 so it is unlikely that she would have gone in for an expensive Silver Ghost so soon afterwards. What is more likely is that she acquired one by adoption, for in 1922 she was married to the son of the 5th Earl of Harewood, Viscount Lascelles. Three years later she ordered a 20 hp, chassis G P K 49. It was a small limousine by Hooper and like most of her subsequent cars it had black wings and dark blue bodywork with the coachline in yellow. There was an extra charge for four-wheel brakes, and should these fail to arrest the car's progress, there was also a first aid kit, which was bound in blue Morocco leather. This was perhaps one of the first instances of this type of equipment being provided in a motor car.

Princess Mary was not granted the title Princess Royal until 1933; the previous holder had been Princess Louise, the eldest daughter of the late King Edward V I I. It is thought that she too might have purchased a 20 hp, chassis G P K 70. However, this had been allocated to the distinguished architect Sir Edwin Lutyens. The continuation sheet shows that the vehicle remained with that profession, because a year after delivery, 1927, it became the property of another member of the Royal Institute of British Architects with whom it remained for close on 20 years.

Princess Arthur of Connaught, daughter-in-law to Queen Victoria's only surviving son at this time (the Duke of Connaught), also purchased a 20 hp in 1925. This was chassis G P K 27 and went to Barkers for the fitment of a cabriolet de ville body. It had four-wheel brakes and was delivered on November 30 that year. Her father-in-law must have been either sceptical of the company or else perfectly satisfied with his Daimlers, because he was nearly 90 when he ordered a Rolls-Royce.

The bigger Rolls-Royce, the Silver Ghost, was modernized in 1925 and emerged as the new Phantom; later to be called the Phantom I. The Prince of Wales ordered a new car almost at once and this was amongst the first series to be built. (Chassis 55 M C had started out as 81 M C, but before long it was changed to the present numbering.) On July 3, 1925 the fully tested chassis left Derby for London and Barkers for the construction of a saloon

Following World War I, Rolls-Royce cars were used more and more frequently by the Royal family – no doubt much to the concern of the Daimler Company. One of Queen Victoria's many grandchildren, Princess Helena Victoria, is about to board a pre-war Silver Ghost after visiting Christ Church, Oxford.

Brought forward:-	910	0	0

CENTRAL GARAGE LTD.   The

LT.COL. THE RT.HON.THE EARL OF HAREWOOD, K.G. D.S.O.
     NEW "HOOPER" ENCLOSED LIMOUSINE, NO.7252.
For 40/50 HP.Rolls-Royce Chassis Phantom II No.84-WJ.

SPECIAL ITEMS. (Contd).

"Hooper" Patent quick-action signal window to off-front door:-	5	10	0
ACCESSORIES. Set of Lucas outside electric lamps, two P.100 Double-Bulb type headlamps, with separate switch on instrument board for small bulbs, two wing lamps, two instrument board lamps, tail lamp, hand inspection lamp, case of spare bulbs; and complete wiring of electric installation. Revised Price:-	35	10	0
Two Lucas electric windscreen wipers, including fitting and wiring. (One additional to estimate):-	5	5	0
Buzzer for communication with driver:-	2	10	0
Miniature speedometer and clock to rear compartment, fitted to centre of "division":-	16	15	0
Cobra bulb horn and bracket:-	6	6	6
Two aluminium number plates and nickel plated licence holder:-	1	11	6
Premier step mat outside each main door:-	2	2	0
Set of loose covers to rear compartment, up to elbow line only:- ✗	14	10	0
Discs to six wheels:-	19	10	0
"Hooper-Fendex" single-bar tubular bumpers to front, and double-bar tubular "C" bumpers to rear, nickel plated finish, including fitting. Revised Price:-	18	5	0
Fog lamp fitted to front dumb iron:-	3	5	0
Pyrene fire extinguisher and bracket:-	3	0	0
Crest, encircled by Garter and surmounted by Coronet, on main doors and back panel:-	8	9	0
Linen cover to protect inside front of rear compartment (for use when luggage is carried inside car):-	Included.		
	1053	9	0
Less 15%:-	158	0	3

LEFT *Detailed quotations such as this for the Hooper coachwork to be fitted to the Earl of Harewood's Phantom II (chassis 84 W J) are unheard of today. Notice in particular such individual fittings as a 'Miniature speedometer and clock to rear compartment' and 'Buzzer for communication with driver'. The car was in fact intended for use by the Earl's wife, Princess Mary, Countess of Harewood.*

RIGHT *Princess Mary visiting Henley-on-Thames in 1930 in her Phantom II (chassis 84 W J) which is displaying the Gilded Canary mascot.*

body. There is a curious note on the file which states: 'This chassis allotted in place of 17 TM, which chassis we are taking back at full price and disposing of as secondhand.' It continues: 'Body ex-17 TM to be fitted to this chassis, with any necessary alterations to scuttle.' Chassis 17 TM was one of the penultimate series in the Silver Ghost range and it is likely that the Company decided to make sure the Prince had a New Phantom as soon as practicable for publicity reasons.

Whatever the thinking behind the change, chassis 55 MC was handed over to the Prince's chauffeur, George Ladbroke, on November 23, 1925. Mr Ladbroke became something of a celebrity later on, having accompanied the Prince in all manner of adventures. These included driving Mrs Simpson (eventually to marry the Prince) across France to seclusion, accompanying them both around France in the late 1930s and – when the 'Phoney War' ended – in a dash into Spain to escape the invading Nazis.

Chassis 55 MC remained with the Prince until November 1929, by which time he had already acquired another New Phantom. This car (chassis 14 RF) was much reported on in the newspapers and in the motoring journals. The Prince forsook Barkers for his coachwork and went to Gurney Nutting for the fitment of a Weymann saloon. This was probably a late decision because at one time Barkers were to be patronized for a sedanca de ville body, but in the end this was abandoned. What had influenced the Prince was that two of his brothers had cars with Gurney Nutting bodywork; the Duke of York had one on his 21 hp Lanchester and

the Duke of Kent also had the same company build him a body for his very fast Bentley Six.

The Prince of Wales obviously took a close interest in this car because he had a great many personal touches added to the coachwork. The saloon had a clever aperture let into the bottom of the Brooks trunk at the rear of the car, which allowed the Prince to slide his golf clubs away. Twin spotlights were fitted either side of the scuttle and an external sun blind forward of the windscreen ran the width of the body, giving the car a very modern appearance. Below this was a small police light, which gave him priority on evening engagements. The coachwork inspectors tested the bodywork at Gurney Nutting and three days later, on January 7, 1928 the guarantee was issued.

Chassis 14 R F was with the Prince for only a short period because just over a year later the car was disposed of to Rolls-Royce for £1,700 to which the Prince added £272 to become one of the first owners of a Phantom II. This new chassis (115 W J) was to be his last. The Phantom II was fairly revolutionary as far as the company was concerned because they had, at last, shed many of the chassis features that had hung on in the Phantom I from the old Silver Ghost. For chassis 115 W J, Gurney Nutting were again entrusted with producing bodywork for the Prince and he chose an enclosed limousine style built to the Weymann principles. This allowed the wooden frames of the body to flex slightly through the use of metal plates rather than rigid wooden joints, and the whole upper portion of the carriage was clothed in a waterproof fabric which made the bodywork very light as well as free from rattles.

One alteration H R H wanted from his previous order was for the nickel parts to be changed where practicable to chromium: for this work Gurney Nutting charged an additional £55. 115 W J was a long-type chassis and at

RIGHT *The 1927 Phantom I Gurney Nutting Weyman Saloon built for H R H The Prince of Wales, who took a great personal interest in its manufacture; as reported in* The Autocar, *January 13, 1928.*

THE PRINCE'S NEW CAR
AND TWO OTHER IMPOSING VEHICLES.

Three 40-50 h.p. New Phantom Rolls-Royce Chassis Fitted with Bodywork Typical of Modern Taste in Automobile Design.

BY putting into commission a 40-50 h.p. New Phantom Rolls-Royce with a Weymann saloon body, H.R.H. the Prince of Wales has undoubtedly set the seal of approval on this type of body construction. It is, moreover, a feather in the cap of the bodybuilders, J. Gurney Nutting and Co., Elystan Street, King's Road, Chelsea, S.W.3, of which they are justifiably proud, that this is the third Weymann saloon which they have supplied to the Royal Family, for the Duke of York is already the owner of a 21 h.p. Lanchester, while Prince George has a Bentley 3, both of which have been fitted with Gurney Nutting Weymann coachwork.

It is typical of the Prince that he has taken a great personal interest in his new car, and has on occasions visited the works to inspect it in various stages of manufacture. Certainly it is a car of which to be proud, for the massive, dignified lines of the radiator and bonnet blend harmoniously with the artistically simple lines of the four-door, four-light body, giving a well-balanced whole in which no part is brought into prominence.

In fact, the car is one at which every keen motorist would instinctively look twice if he saw it on the road, but it attracts attention by its line alone, for the colour scheme could not be in quieter taste.

From stem to stern the car is black, except for a red line on the wheel discs and the faint blue sheen of the chromium-plated fittings. The domed wings have the side lamps moulded into them, and the two-pane vertical screen has its lower edge curved to conform to the outline of the scuttle, giving the driver a particularly good view of the road, and allowing him to see the front wings. A spotlight is fitted in each of the lower corners of the windscreen, and buffers are fitted at front and rear. A large Brooks trunk has extensible sides so that it can, if need be, contain golf clubs.

In the interior the same quiet taste is displayed, while the seats are designed to afford the maximum degree of comfort, so that even on a long run the occupant should experience no feeling other than of restfulness. The rear compartment is upholstered in biscuit-coloured cloth, and the main seat has permanent arm rests at the sides, with a folding arm rest in the middle, which, when down, transforms the seat into the equivalent of two comfortable armchairs. At the back of the front seat is a rising and falling partition equipped with a winding gear particularly

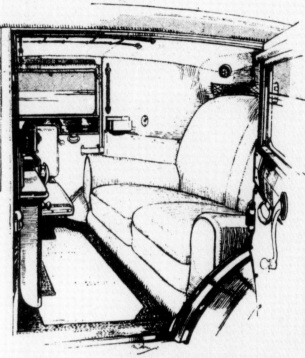
Almost severely simple, although comfortable, is the interior of the Prince's new car.

The Gurney Nutting Weymann saloon which has been built for the Prince of Wales.

LEFT *Unlike other members of the Royal Family, Prince George would often drive himself to public events, with his equerry sitting beside him. The official driver would be relegated to the back seat! Prince George is alighting from the front of his Phantom III (chassis 3 AZ 43) at Tunbridge Wells, shortly before World War II. As a point of interest, drivers of many of the older Rolls-Royce cars would almost invariably exit from the car via the front passenger's seat; this was to avoid the obstructions of the right-hand gear lever and hand brake lever which could often make leaving via the driver's door a little awkward.*

LEFT *The Duke of Kent also liked to drive long distances. Here, along with the Duchess, he is seen at the wheel of his Phantom III on a visit to Vienna in 1938.*

the request of the owner Rolls-Royce reduced the distance between the pedals and the rim of the steering wheel by lengthening the pedal shafts; this was more than likely to allow the Prince to drive, for he was not very tall and may have experienced some difficulty with other cars. The Prince of Wales staff received the car from a representative of Gurney Nutting in December 1929 and it remained with him until June 1931, when it was acquired by a resident of Mayfair. By then, the Prince had other diversions, mainly American ones, because it was about this time that Mrs Wallis Simpson came into his life.

From then onwards the Prince tended to choose vehicles of a more transatlantic flavour such as Humbers (much influenced by developments in North America) and, particularly, Buicks (which were assembled for the Prince at the American firm's Canadian factory). With his attention turning to other matters, Rolls-Royce probably realized that they had lost the chance to wean the heir to the throne away from Daimler, but the company could still claim considerable patronage amongst other members of the Royal Family – and it was growing.

It had continued in 1928 with the delivery to Princess Victoria of yet another 20 hp, this time chassis G X L 15. The Princess was the sister of King George V and she resided in Iver, Buckinghamshire. Her Park Ward limousine was painted blue and black and had started life as a company stock vehicle. In the spring of 1933 she sold the car and immediately took delivery of a more powerful 20/25 hp model. But this is to anticipate another delivery, one made to Princess Mary, the wife of the by now Earl of Harewood. Her order for the Phantom II must have been made at about the same time as that for the Prince of Wales because the chassis allocated is just a few numbers earlier, 84 W J. This car, ordered through Rippon Bros in Huddersfield, was sold on September 24, 1929 with delivery promised as soon as possible: in the event, the instruction book on the car was sent to the coachbuilders on December 3 that year. Hooper were responsible for the enclosed limousine body with division. All the interior fittings were in silver plate and this included a speedometer and clock to the rear compartment. Like the previous 20 hp, the car was painted with black wings and dark blue body picked out in a lighter blue and fine-lined in yellow.

Princess Victoria took delivery of her 20/25 chassis, GWZ 9, in April 1933, having ordered it the previous Christmas. The completed vehicle sported a Park Ward enclosed limousine body, as had her previous car. With the old car taken in part exchange and the special allowance made, the total sum deducted from the price of the 20/25 was £730 – a not inconsiderable sum. The Princess very obviously took a great interest in what was going on at Park Ward's factory at Willesden and her requirements fill several pages. Amongst them was an RAC badge moved to the radiator cap, a Bosch two-note horn, a 'V' and a crown on each rear door, blinds to all windows, an octagonal clock transferred from the old 20 hp and – somewhat curiously – a crown on a shield to be fitted at the back end of the bonnet, rather than to the roof as normal. Sadly, Princess Victoria did not have a great deal of time left to enjoy her new car and its unusual fitments as she died in December 1935, her brother's Jubilee Year.

By now the younger sons of George V were settling into their rounds of public duties and all except the Prince of Wales were married. But 1936 was to see three kings – King George V, who died at the end of January; King Edward VIII who abdicated before the year was out, and King George VI, who succeeded him.

King George VI's two younger brothers were very much motoring men. Prince Henry, indeed, was a most practical motorist and must have been amongst the first to realize that gloss paintwork on bonnets and the like can produce distorting effects. He had all his ceremonial cars painted with shiny black wings and a dull matt finish elsewhere.

The mighty V12 Rolls-Royce Phantom III was announced at the October 1935 Olympia Motor Show and the Duke of Kent ordered his car in April the following year. A special allowance of £500 was deducted from the chassis price, which came to £1,850. The steering column was set at a lower angle than usual (an 'F' setting) and was $2\frac{1}{2}$ inches longer than normal. Barkers were directed to build a sports saloon with division on the chassis, 3 AZ 43, and it arrived at their works on June 17.

The Duke had the coachbuilders fit quite a number of extras, amongst them a chromium-plated instrument board and finishers, Marchal side and headlamps, a chromium-plated luggage rack to the rear boot lid and blinds

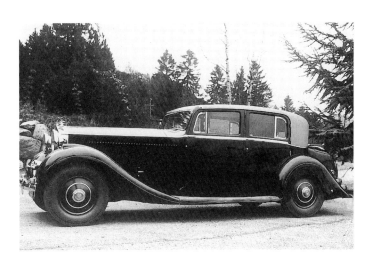

BELOW AND CENTRE
RIGHT *The Duke of
Gloucester's Barker-bodied
Phantom III (chassis 3 AX
195) photographed in 1973,
some twenty years after it
passed into private hands.
It was then owned by a
Mr Benge.*

ABOVE *Phantom III chassis 3 AZ 43, which was made for
The Duke of Kent in 1936, now in Switzerland. Its present
owner has had the car completely restored to pristine condition.*

RIGHT *Prior to delivery the
Duke of Gloucester's Rolls-
Royce 25/30 was photographed
by the body makers H. J.
Mulliner – the suppliers were
The Car Mart Ltd of London.*

HRH The Duchess of Gloucester arrives in her new 25/30 hp at Lord's Cricket Ground for the Eton and Harrow match in the summer of 1937.

to the division and rear quarter windows. Unusually, he chose not to have a heater but in case HRH chose to drive himself, the front seats had armrests each side, with a folding armrest in between; the outboard rests containing 'companions.' In motoring terms, companions are small receptacles (often veneered) and containing items such as a light, mirror, scent bottles, cigars or cigarettes, lighter, and even writing implements.

The Duke, who envisaged using the car abroad, had a sunshine roof fitted as well as an American police siren, and a headlamp dimming device adjustable from the steering column and operated by a foot switch. The file requested 'Special attention to performance'. The car was handed over on June 17, 1936, and up to the outbreak of the Second World War received regular attention at the London Service Centre at Claremont Road, and after 1940 at Hythe Road. It was finished in black with a black fabric roof covering and chromium plated mouldings; the interior was finished in pigskin. For public duties the driver could affix a shield above the centre of the windscreen.

Chassis 3 AZ 43 remained with the Duke until his death during the War when the car was transferred to the Duchess, Princess Marina, in whose care it remained until replaced by a postwar model in the spring of 1949. At that time it was disposed of for £1,750, £100 less than the normal original purchase price.

1937 must have been an expensive year for the Duke of Gloucester, for that year Prince Henry ordered two Rolls-Royces, one a 25/30 hp and the other, like his brother's, a Phantom III. The order for the new Phantom was made in December 1936 and the Duke was fortunate in gaining £50 more allowance than his brother as a special discount; he was also awarded 20 per cent off the total price of the body extras, but bearing in mind he was purchasing two cars in one year is perhaps understandable that Rolls-Royce were generous. Barkers were entrusted with the building of the enclosed limousine, which was to be painted in the matt black finish with only the wings in a gloss paint.

Prince Henry chose a multitude of additional fitments and it is really only possible to mention a few of them from the chassis card of 3 AX 195. The six months body construction time was spent in fitting the following:

special 'F' steering column as fitted to his brother's car, a Clayton heater, two-tone horn with loud and soft controls on the steering wheel, louvred glass to all door and quarter light windows to prevent draughts, pneumatic and pleated upholstery to seats and squabs, a windscreen spray, a cloth pad to cover the small rear window when required, a roof heraldic shield light, a reversing light, a Philco radio set, rear quarter-light purdah windows on a sliding channel to cover clear glass as needed, reading lamps in the quarters, a sunshine roof, a klaxon horn, an umbrella in a fitted aluminium cover under the front seat, swivelling headlamp mechanism, silk blinds to the division and main windows, detachable and adjustable armrests for the front doors, twin Stephen Grebel spotlights on either side of windscreen, and the woodwork in plain walnut throughout.

The Duke's chauffeur, Mr Rhodes, took delivery of the completed Phantom I I I from Barkers on May 1, 1937, the final price being only £14 short of £3,000, an enormous sum for those days. Chassis 3 A X 195, however, was to cover prodigious mileages both in the United Kingdom and later in Australia when the Duke became Governor-General.

The 25/30 hp ordered at the same time as the Phantom I I I was chassis G U N 35 and again this had a limousine body, although in this case built by H. J. Mulliner. Many special items again found their way into the coachwork, and they echoed those fitted to the big V12 Phantom. The completed car was registered C L L 789 and was used more by the Duchess than her husband. For recognition at night the little blue light was mounted to the left of the heraldic shield; why it was not centrally located is not recorded. With its black fabric roof and the very distinctive paint scheme, the car looked particularly smart on the smaller chassis. It was handed over to its owner in early 1937.

However, with the announcement of the new Wraith with its independent front suspension in 1938, the Duke decided to change his car.

HRH The Duke of Connaught's Park Ward-bodied Wraith
(chassis WRB6) photographed in 1939.

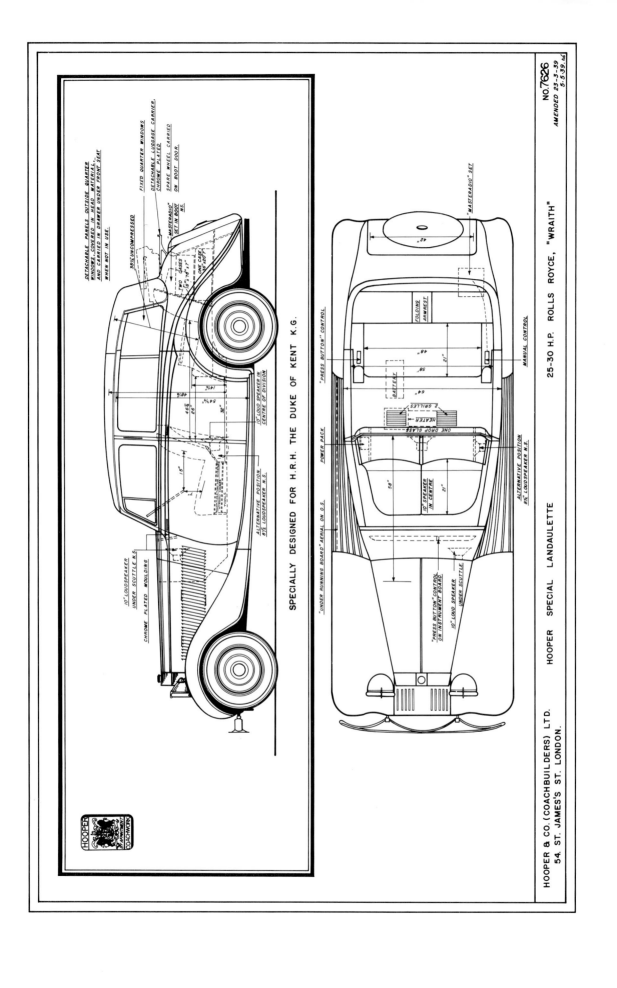

SPECIALLY DESIGNED FOR H.R.H. THE DUKE OF KENT K.G.

HOOPER & CO. (COACHBUILDERS) LTD.   HOOPER SPECIAL LANDAULETTE   25-30 H.P. ROLLS ROYCE, "WRAITH"
54. ST. JAMES'S ST. LONDON.

NO.7626
AMENDED 23-3-39
5-5-39

This time Thrupp & Maberly were given the coachwork order for chassis W M B 62 and again most of the fitments that H R H had requested on his earlier car were repeated. A gun turret mascot was transferred to the new Wraith, but the number plate was new – F X R 888. It was also to appear on his postwar cars. Chassis W M B 62, which was delivered in late 1938, was one of three Royal Wraiths, the second being based on chassis W R B 6.

W R B 6 had been ordered in November 1938 by the 88-year-old Duke of Connaught, the last remaining son of Queen Victoria. It must have been pretty galling for Daimler to learn that Rolls-Royce had acquired the Duke's patronage as all his motoring life he had owned Daimlers. They may have been even more distressed to learn that the elderly Duke was allowed to trade in his old Daimler and was also to be given an allowance of £350 for his custom. With both these credits Rolls-Royce sold the chassis for quite a reasonable sum.

The Duke also forsook Hooper for the Rolls-Royce owned coach-builders Park Ward. This company, which was taken over by the car makers in 1939, produced a standard enclosed limousine with black-painted wings and the lower panels, scuttle and bonnet in Royal Lake. The upholstery was in plain cloth at the rear and black leather at the front. The Duke appreciated the comforts of life and purchased the optional heater, along with an armrest to the front seat door, a bracket and standard holder for State use and crests to be fitted 'as on the Daimler car'. The completed vehicle was handed over to Captain Fitzroy Fyers, M V O, Equerry to H R H, on March 7, 1939.

With the Duke's death in 1942 it was acquired by Prince Henry, Duke of Gloucester and it sailed to Australia in 1945 when he took up his Governor-Generalship. All three cars returned in 1947: the old Duke's Wraith was disposed of shortly afterwards to Standard-Triumph Cars of

Finely detailed drawing of the very last Royal Rolls-Royce to be supplied before World War II, a Hooper-bodied 25/30 Wraith.

Grosvenor Square in London, in part exchange for a Triumph Renown. When last heard of it was in Ontario and a non-runner.

The final Rolls-Royce to be built for a member of the Royal Family prior to the Second World War went to the Duke of Kent. His was ordered in April 1939 and delivered at the end of September. Chassis W H C 2 was fitted with a special landaulette body by Hooper and was painted in black, relieved by a chromium plated moulding. There was plain fawn cloth to the rear seat and doors and pigskin to the front compartment, as on the Phantom I I I owned by the Duke.

The Hooper landaulette was fitted with a heater and a radio, which had speakers in both front and rear compartments. Detachable rear quarter-light covers were kept under the front seat and there was the usual fitment to the front roof canopy for flying the Duke's standard. Once again Prince George specified 'particular attention to be paid to acceleration'. Because of the radio, heater and special Marchal headlamps a request was put in for the dynamo to give maximum output; additional undershields were ordered to keep the engine compartment clean. The car became Princess Marina's on the death of her husband in 1942 and it remained with her household until the autumn of 1949 when it was replaced by a postwar Silver Wraith.

The outbreak of the Second World War occurring only a matter of days before this Wraith had been delivered meant that Rolls-Royce had concluded their building of cars for the Royal Family for the immediate future. But the goodwill they had fostered and their cars' reliable service and exclusivity had laid a foundation that would bear fruit in the postwar years, including the ultimate accolade in the British motor industry: 'Motor Car Manufacturers to Her Majesty The Queen'.

The Hooper offices and showrooms. (Inset) *The Duchess of Kent arriving at Rochester in Kent in late 1946 in her Hooper-bodied Wraith.*

3

THE MOVE AWAY FROM DAIMLER

To acquire the Royal Warrant of Appointment is a notable achievement, but in most cases it does little for sales. However, to lose the honour usually conveys to the general public an impression of a lowering of standards by the concern involved which can be measurably bad for business.

The last Daimler to leave the Palace on official duties was in 1960, the year that BSA disposed of their subsidiary to Jaguar Cars Ltd. Jaguar made no secret of the fact that essentially all they wanted was the floor space at the Daimler Radford works for expansion. The last Daimler-designed body and engine was the Majestic Major, which finally disappeared in 1968. Since then the only recognizable Daimler has really been the DS 420 Limousine, which continues to sell in healthy numbers, though production ends in 1992. This car has had a number of minor improvements over the years, but is essentially the same as when introduced in 1968.

Why did Daimler fall from Royal favour? There were a number of explanations put forward which, although not individually enough to warrant banishment, together were quite devastating. Failure to produce sufficiently marketable cars, or to keep in check the activities of a Chairman and his wife bent on aggrandizement, failure to maintain the distinction between the carriage trade and the general motoring public, and an inability to encourage sufficient capital investment, all played their part.

Daimler had been acquired by Birmingham Small Arms in 1910 and in its 50-year association BSA could not have made a great deal of profit from its purchase. It was said that the Daimler overdraft in the early 1930s was so frighteningly large that its creditors were anxious to call it in for fear of losing their money altogether.

Overseeing the postwar period at BSA was its Chairman, Sir Bernard Docker, who in 1949 had married Lady Norah Collins, whose husband had died a short time beforehand. The new Lady Docker set out to make her impression on society, and along with her husband she took an intense interest in Daimler; within two years the couple were the centre of attraction at the Earls Court Motor Show with their exotically extravagant personal cars. To advance her cause Lady Docker had herself voted on to the board of Hooper, which since 1940 had also been a part of BSA.

For some five years this couple dominated the annual London Motor Show in a quite bizarre way. The Lady Docker Sports Saloon, the Gold Daimler, the Sir Bernard Special Fixed Head Coupe, Lady Docker's Silver Flash Coupe, the fabulous Stardust Limousine and finally, in 1955, the Ivory White Zebra Coupe, all were aimed at creating headlines and publicity for the Daimler name – and the Chairman and his wife.

This continuing display of unbridled wealth was eventually to be the subject of a boardroom battle at BSA, culminating in the removal of the Chairman and his wife. Financial wrangles accompanied their departure, there were currency disputes with the British Treasury and then came Lady Docker's highly publicized row with the authorities of Monte Carlo. One may assume that Daimler's most prestigious customers were not terribly amused to be driving around in cars associated with such an outrageous lifestyle. Although Sir Bernard had enjoyed an *entrée* to Royal circles in the 1940s with the late King, his company, and certainly that of his wife, was neither sought nor particularly enjoyed by the new residents at Buckingham Palace. It would be ridiculous to suggest that this antipathy was enough to precipitate the fall from favour of the Daimler name in the Royal Mews, but it may well have been the last straw.

From 1953–1955 Daimler did not produce a limousine chassis. The renowned Straight Eight had ceased in Coronation year and it was succeeded two years later by a chassis that did nothing to improve on the old design. The new DK 400 had a straight-six engine and although robust and fast for its day was still coupled to a pre-selector gearbox and this was placed in a chassis that was unworthy of the Coventry firm. For Daimler, who had founded their reputation on limousine chassis, the two-year gap and the poor reception for the new DK 400 was to be fatal.

An idea of the drop in interest in the Coventry product can be gauged from the fact that during the runs of the old limousine chassis more than 40 units a year were going through the works. After 1955 they were lucky to attract 20 a year! So bad was the situation that by 1959 production was abandoned and it was not until 1961, under Jaguar auspices, that another limousine (the Majestic Major) was in production. Meanwhile, production at Rolls-Royce was much healthier; in the period 1946 to 1959 they produced a total of 1,783 limousine chassis. From 1946–53 Daimlers produced a mere 273.

ABOVE RIGHT *As early as the first year of the new Queen's reign, her Majesty seemed keen to set a new style in motor transport. Here on a Coronation visit to the Royal Navy in 1953, Her Majesty travels by Rolls-Royce with her late father George VI's Straight-Eight Daimler as the second car.*

BELOW RIGHT *A pair of ex-Royal Daimlers pictured here when owned by the Author. Both have bodies by Hooper, on DK 400 chassis; on the left is a limousine, the other is a landaulette (the hood over the rear seat can fold). They were no match – so far as the quality of their chassis were concerned – for their Rolls-Royce rivals.*

BELOW *After a quarter of a century a Daimler returned to the Royal Mews in 1987, although only 'on hire' and not as a vehicle owned by the Palace. This DS 420 model is now one of a pair, often used by junior members of the Royal Family.*

53

Rolls-Royce had always thought that the acquisition of the Royal Warrant would be a fitting acknowledgement of their achievements in the motoring field. They had long claimed to produce the Best Car in the World but the world's most renowned Royal Family had chosen to shop elsewhere for their motor transport. In 1947 Princess Elizabeth was married to Prince Philip of Greece. Prince Philip's uncle was Lord Mountbatten, who had been an admirer of Rolls-Royce cars for some 25 years, and no doubt he conveyed his enthusiasm to the young couple . . .

In 1948 the Duke of Edinburgh was invited to the new Rolls-Royce factory at Crewe in Cheshire. This had been a 'shadow factory' during the war but had now taken over motor car production whilst Derby concentrated on aeroplane engines. It was during this visit that the Duke encountered the experimental straight-eight engined Bentley. This engine was one of three military type engines which were in straight-four, six and eight-cylinder configurations, B40, B60 and B80. The B80 Bentley was used for a variety of motoring experiments and was renowned for its startling performance, so much so that it earned the nickname 'Scalded Cat'. The young Duke asked if he could borrow it and indeed he had the car for a week. He also learned that there was a similarly-engined car using a Rolls-Royce radiator which was of altogether more sophisticated construction. This particular car had been built for the Chairman of Rolls-Royce, later to be given a Peerage as Lord Hives. It had been fitted with long-range tanks to enable it to travel between Rolls-Royce's other shadow factories at Glasgow and Derby without re-fuelling.

At that time Rolls-Royce were by no means sure that they should enter into direct competition with Daimler who had a similar configuration engine in a limousine chassis. The Park Ward Rolls-Royce straight-eight had been fitted with a close-coupled four-door saloon body and the Duke of Edinburgh was impressed enough to ask if the company would consider building him a car on a similar chassis. The management realized that a car owned by the Consort to the Heiress Presumptive was the opportunity they needed. Perhaps it would only be a matter of time before the half-century of Daimler supremacy at the Palace was under threat. So they agreed to the Duke's request.

4

THE DUKE OF EDINBURGH'S CHOICE

'THE MAHARAJAH OF NABHA'
Phantom IV 4 AF 2

Tʜᴇ ᴠᴇʀʏ sᴘᴇᴄɪᴀʟ ᴄᴀʀ that Rolls-Royce built to the order of The Duke of Edinburgh was given the straight-eight engine that had so impressed him on his visit to the company's factory in 1948. The Rolls-Royce board restricted production of the 12 ft 1 in wheelbase chassis to just 17 and with one exception ownership was to be confined to heads of state and members of the British Royal Family. The exception was the Chairman of the company, Lord Hives. After two and a half years this car, chassis 4 AF 12, was refurbished for Princess Marina but during his ownership Lord Hives enjoyed the unique distinction of being the only person outside these two exalted groups who owned a Phantom IV.

The Duke's car, chassis 4 AF 2 was built to his specification but he was given advice on its construction from Rolls-Royce, H. J. Mulliner and the motor car retailers Car Mart Ltd. At the time of the order the Duke and his wife, HRH Princess Elizabeth, the Duchess of Edinburgh, had only recently taken delivery of a 27 hp Daimler Limousine, which had been purchased for them out of contributions made by the RAF and the WAAF towards a wedding present at the time of their marriage in November 1947. This Daimler DE 27 was delivered to Clarence House, the couple's London residence, on February 2, 1948. It was a short while afterwards that the Duke made the visit to Rolls-Royce that made him an enthusiast of the marque.

After consultation between the interested parties in the summer of 1948 the order for the Phantom IV was confirmed on November 15 that year. The customer code selected to preserve secrecy whilst the car was going through the works was 'Maharajah of Nabha'. Why this Indian Prince was chosen is difficult to know for sure, apart from the fact that he was a keen motorist and a collector of vintage cars.

Years later, in March 1965, Prince Philip came face-to-face with the real Maharajah at the wild life bird sanctuary at Bharatpur in India. However it is unlikely that the Duke had any idea that this eminent Maharajah's name had been used to ensure the confidentiality of his first Rolls-Royce.

The construction of chassis 4 AF 2 seems to have been entirely at the behest of the Duke, as his arms, encircled by the ribbon of the Order of the Garter, appear at the top of the coachbuilder's line drawing. The people involved in advising the Duke were Jack Scott the senior man at the sales department of Rolls-Royce at Conduit Street in London, H. T. Johnstone, the managing director of H. J. Mulliner, and A. P. Field, the general manager of Car Mart Ltd.

The Duke of Edinburgh's own interest in the first car to be built exclusively for him is confirmed by the visits he made to the drawing office at the coachbuilders. The Phantom IV was actually built in the setting-out shop at H. J. Mulliner; nowadays that would probably be known as an experimental department. It was here that the full-size drawing was converted into patterns and jigs for manufacture of the wood and metal components. Years later, the son of the Mulliner managing director, who followed his father into the firm, recalled his first encounter with the car in early 1949. His work was to help in the making of the aluminium covers for

The H. J. Mulliner-bodied Rolls-Royce Phantom IV supplied by The Car Mart Ltd to Their Royal Highnesses The Princess Elizabeth and The Duke of Edinburgh.

the spare wheels mounted either side of the bonnet, and he remembers the very high standard of craftsmanship that went into this particular body; no detail was spared.

Whilst all the preparatory work was going on at the Fulham works of H. J. Mulliner, the straight-eight-engined Phantom IV was being prepared at the Rolls-Royce experimental workshops at the Clan Foundry, Belper, near Derby. The completed chassis was sent to London on July 20, 1949 with delivery promised to Clarence House exactly a year later. The interior dimensions of the Phantom were to be repeated in all subsequent Royal Rolls-Royces built for the use of the future Queen, apart from the rear doors which were an exceptionally generous 3 ft 2 in. As the car was not built as a State Limousine it was fitted with number plates which, in the fashion of the day, were fitted below the boot lid and integral with the bodywork, with illumination for them concealed behind the plates.

The man who carried the responsibility for translating all the ideas to reality was Mulliner's technical director Stanley Watts. His classic razor-edged design has survived over 40 years surprisingly well. The wheelbase of the Phantom was 12 ft 1 in, only 2 in shorter than the Daimler Straight Eights then in use at the Palace, which had the longest car wheelbase then in production in Britain, or indeed in Europe generally. The engine, of 5,675 cc, produced an estimated 170 bhp (traditionally Rolls-Royce do not disclose the power output of their engines) whilst the Daimler of a similar configuration produced 150 bhp from 5,460 cc with twin S U carburettors;

the Rolls-Royce had only a single Stromberg carburettor. The transmission as originally fitted to the Rolls-Royce was a manual four-speed gearbox, with the gear lever fitted into a cutaway close to the driver's seat on his right side. Other features of the chassis included a 23-gallon fuel tank with a further 4 gallons in reserve and a heavy-duty generator which coped with the electrical load on the 78 amp/hour battery; other Phantoms managed on a 55 amp/hour battery. When alternators became fashionable, a study by Peter Pedrick, the senior electrician at Rolls-Royce, suggested that the charging rate of the old generator was well up to the loading imposed on it, and its replacement with an alternator was considered to offer such minor gain at speed as to be not worthwhile. Indeed, Mr Pedrick discovered that the old dynamo cut in at processional speeds earlier than the alternator then being considered. His recommendation, still in the car's file, was a curt 'leave strictly alone.'

But it was the bodywork which aroused most public interest when the car was revealed to the press. The Duke of Edinburgh clearly had in mind that he would drive the car himself from time to time. His father-in-law King George VI's postwar Daimler Straight Eights were all fitted with a bucket seat formation to the front compartment in case His Majesty should wish to drive himself; and sometimes the Duke would drive the Daimler 27 hp that he and the Duchess had been given after their wedding. To accommodate his tall frame, the Duke's Phantom IV's steering was raked for owner/driver use, the seat itself was adjusted forwards and rearwards, and the front seat had inboard and outboard armrests. These arrangements, which were coupled with a separate heating control and a radio volume switch, gave rather more comfort than one would have expected on a limousine of the period. The Duke certainly drove the car with some verve and as later engineers working on the car recollect, it was not unusual for the car to arrive for routine maintenance at the coachbuilders mud-spattered from fast driving.

It must have been in Their Royal Highnesses' minds to use the car overseas from time to time because the speedometer was gradated both in mph and kmh and the huge Lucas headlamps could be switched for either left- or right-hand driving.

ABOVE *The 1947 wedding gift Daimler had a varied career after being displaced by the Rolls-Royce. By 1988 it was residing in the suburbs of New York. It is seen here looking a little less than regal, but the clamp on the roof for the shield and Royal standard can still be made out.*

OVERLEAF *Just prior to delivery to the Heiress Presumptive and her husband, the Phantom IV was photographed in Gunnersbury Park (MAIN PICTURE). Most of the publicity photographs of the car were taken from a similar angle, so that the numberplate was not obvious.*
The car was built with manual transmission – note the clutch pedal (Inset LEFT). Five years later it was replaced by a General Motors automatic transmission. The stalk to the right of the steering column carries the switch for the old type semaphore trafficators – these too have been replaced. As to the interior, (Inset, RIGHT) the absence of a rear door pillar helped to give the rear compartment a spacious appearance – in contrast to the very heavy look of the State Daimlers.

A nautical touch was provided by a compass, but it was probably the power operation of many of the facilities that interested members of the Royal Family when the car was finally delivered. The windows were activated electrically, as were the division, the shutter to the glass section in the roof over the rear compartment, the rear window blind and the radio aerial. Heating and ventilation was quite the most comprehensive arranged to that date. The two front chromium plated grilles beneath the headlamps provided air intakes to three heaters, one for the front compartment situated under the facia, and the other two under the front and rear seats for feeding warm air to the rear compartment. In addition there was a pipe which picked up warm air from the back of the radiator and fed it to the windscreen capping rail for demisting purposes, and this, coupled with screenwash equipment, was a boon in inclement weather.

As the car was a dual purpose vehicle, for use on both public and private engagements, the lighting to the rear compartment was important and four interior lights were fitted which, coupled with a strip light for public engagements, meant that a good view of the occupants was provided when the occasion demanded.

A powerful Radiomobile 4020 set was installed at the front of the centre armrest of the rear seat and this had a speaker set into the cabinet which was placed centrally behind the division. The division cabinet also contained a clock which swivelled for winding and correction, an ashtray, a heater outlet and a lockable magazine rack. Also in the centre armrest, behind the radio, was a lid which when lifted revealed a fitted mirror, notepaper and writing implements. Minor vanity sets were fitted in the quarter-light trim above the rear seat armrests, below discreet reading lights.

Cross-band figured walnut veneer was carried through to both front and rear compartments and this complemented the green leather seats and trim of the front compartment and the light Liebman Grey cloth to the rear. The carpet to the rear was a curly mohair rug with a plain silk pile border, the front having green carpeting and sorbo rubber over-mats.

Externally, the car was painted in a darkish green colour and it seems as if the choice was made by the Princess. Both Queen Mary and her daughter, The Princess Royal, favoured green for their cars. The particular shade was given the name Valentine Green, but whether this reference to the company that mixed the paint or was a romantic reference is not known. So that the car should be recognized at night, a small blue police light was fitted centrally above the windscreen and behind this, a few inches away, a plug was let into the roof of the car which, when removed, could be replaced by the Royal couple's personal heraldic shield and standard. No heraldic decoration was painted on the rear doors or the boot lid, presumably because when on private matters the car would be less easily recognized without them; also, the rear quarter windows had blanking panels to restrict the view into the rear compartment.

At last, on July 6, 1950, after the general manager of Car Mart, A. P. Field, and a representative from Rolls-Royce had inspected the car and were satisfied, it was driven to Clarence House where it was handed over to the Duke of Edinburgh and Princess Elizabeth; it bore the registration number LGO 10.

The young couple's Daimler 27 hp, which had been registered H R H 1, was disposed of shortly after the death of King George VI in early 1952; meanwhile Rolls-Royce could celebrate the fact that once again they had an owner in the heir to the Throne.

Sadly for the Royal couple, their relative privacy was to last but a short time. The Duke's naval career had had to be curtailed as the King's increasing disability laid rather more responsibilities than he would have wished on his young daughter's and her husband's shoulders. The first Phantom I V's time as a private vehicle was not to last long. In the first week of February 1952, King George VI died peacefully in his sleep at Sandringham House. He was a mere 56 years of age.

At the time the Heiress Presumptive to the Throne and her husband were in East Africa. At once arrangements were made to fly Her Majesty and the Duke of Edinburgh home as quickly as possible. In the gathering gloom of the afternoon following the King's death, the BOAC Argonaut touched down at London Airport. After the aircraft had taxied into position, the assembled dignatories, led by Prime Minster Winston Churchill, waited whilst the aircraft steps were brought up. A short distance away stood the tall, sombre Daimlers sent by the Crown Equerry from the

Royal Mews. Descending the aircraft steps it must have seemed as if the undertakers has sent the cars to the airport, such was the impression they made. At Clarence House, the Rolls-Royce Phantom IV, which represented a more carefree existence, languished in the garage . . .

With so much to do in the coming weeks it was some time before attention could be turned to deciding which cars would be allocated to the new monarch and which would become the property of HM Queen Elizabeth the Queen Mother. Of the State Daimlers, only one 1949 Straight Eight (chassis 51741) was taken over by the Queen Mother. Her Majesty Queen Elizabeth acquired two pre-war Straight Eight-engined Lanchester cars, a limousine and a landaulette, as well as the King's Hooper-bodied drophead $2\frac{1}{2}$-litre coupe. This left for official purposes three matching State Landaulettes, all Daimler Straight Eights, one from 1949 and the other two from 1947. It was to be a severe jolt to Daimler who through their holding company BSA, heard that Hooper & Co, (also a part of BSA) had been commanded to prepare the Rolls-Royce Phantom IV as a State car.

The new monarch undertook no public engagements for two months following her accession. Meanwhile, chassis 4 AF 2 was at Hoopers – much to the disappointment of H. J. Mulliner. However it was felt that Hooper & Co were more familiar with the requirements of the State cars: after all, they had built them for nigh on half a century.

There was quite a lot of work to be undertaken, apart from repainting from Valentine Green to Royal Claret over black. The front compartment had to be retrimmed in dark blue cloth, the registration plates removed from front and rear and the area which held the rear plate filled in and painted over. Finally, C. G. Francis was called to Hoopers to paint the heraldry on to the rear doors and the boot lid.

The completed Rolls-Royce State car undertook its first public engagement along with the new Queen, on April 10, 1952 when Her Majesty distributed Maundy Money to the elderly recipients at Westminster Abbey. Rolls-Royce had achieved what they had hoped for for so many years, one of their cars was in the State fleet at Buckingham Palace.

The Rolls-Royce Phantom IV soon became a favourite at the Palace,

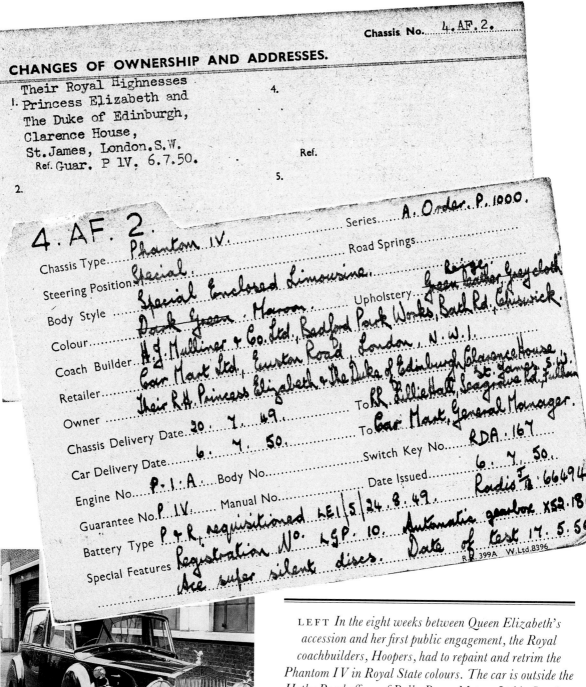

Chassis No. 4.AF.2.

CHANGES OF OWNERSHIP AND ADDRESSES.

Their Royal Highnesses
1. Princess Elizabeth and
The Duke of Edinburgh,
Clarence House,
St.James, London. S.W.
  Ref. Guar. P 1V. 6.7.50.

4.

Ref.

5.

2.

4.AF.2.

Series.....A.Order.P.1000.

Chassis Type.....Phantom. IV.

Road Springs.....

Steering Position.....Special.

Body Style.....Special Enclosed Limousine.

Upholstery.....Green leather grey cloth

Colour.....Dark Green. Maroon.

Coach Builder.....H.J. Mulliner + Co. Ltd., Bedford Park Works, Bath Rd. Chiswick.

Retailer.....Car Mart Ltd., Euston Road, London, N.W.1.

Owner.....Their R.H. Princess Elizabeth + the Duke of Edinburgh Clarence House. To RR. Lillie Hall, Seagrave Rd. Fulham St. James S.W. To Car Mart, General Manager.

Chassis Delivery Date.....20. 7. 49.

Car Delivery Date.....6. 7. 50.

Switch Key No.....RDA.167.

Engine No.....P.1.A. Body No.....

Date Issued.....6. 7. 50.

Guarantee No. P.1V. Manual No.....

Radio J.B. 66494.

Battery Type.....P + R. requisitioned LE1/5/24.8.49.

Automatic gearbox X52.184

Special Features.....Registration No. LGP.10. Ace super silent discs. Date of test 17.5.50.

R.R.399A W.Ltd.8396

LEFT *In the eight weeks between Queen Elizabeth's accession and her first public engagement, the Royal coachbuilders, Hoopers, had to repaint and retrim the Phantom IV in Royal State colours. The car is outside the Hythe Road offices of Rolls-Royce Motors Ltd in London.* ABOVE *As a company, Rolls-Royce has always kept detailed records of every car it makes – the Royal cars, of course, being no exception. This is some of the recorded information regarding chassis 4 A F 2. Amongst other details mentioned is the change of colour and the fitment of the automatic gearbox.*

acquiring a higher rate of average mileage than the State Daimlers as it was elevated to become the No 1 State car. By early 1955 it had run up well over 30,000 miles when it was taken to the London Service Centre at Hythe Road for a service check. The opportunity was taken to replace the manual gearbox with the Hydramatic automatic gearbox, this unit having been

BELOW LEFT *Designed in the 1940s, but still giving faithful service in the 1990s, the Phantom IV 4 AF 2. Unlike its later sister Phantom IV, 4 BP 5, it has only once been overseas. That was in 1977 when it was flown by the RAF to West Germany for the Queen's Silver Jubilee Parade given by the British Army of The Rhine.*

BELOW RIGHT *The interior of the Phantom IV as it appeared in 1990. It remains impressive, although much refurbishment has been carried out during its four decades of Royal service. The Coronation Coach is in the background.*

introduced as an option to Rolls-Royce customers in late 1952. The company was probably quite pleased to do this as the natural resonance of the big $5\frac{1}{2}$-litre engine had caused problems with crankshaft balance. Around this time the semaphore-type trafficator arms were withdrawn and the new flashing indicators fitted; rear reflectors were also added.

A year later, in early 1956, whilst The Queen was in Africa, the type of internally-illuminated shield was fitted, which required alterations to the roof plug to allow the power to reach the shield. At the same time an aperture was made behind the shield plug to accommodate the new type of flagmast which, like that fitted to Princess Margaret's Phantom IV, could be pushed up through a trapdoor in the roof, thus avoiding the need for the chauffeur or detective to get out of the car and erect the standard, as on the old cars. Mechanically, little was altered apart from the fitment of a full-flow oil filter to replace the old style bypass system.

In its first 40 years this Phantom IV has covered something approaching 200,000 miles. Up to the arrival of the Phantom Vs in 1960 and 1961 it was averaging around 6,000 miles a year, but following their arrival and that of the Phantom IV Landaulette, its annual mileage dropped to around half of that and is now even less.

Like all working vehicles – and the Royal Mews insist that the cars are used almost daily – the Phantom IV 4 AF 2 is kept in good working order and has been modified to take cognisance of the new regulations that have come into force since the car was constructed. The headlights, for instance, were changed to sealed-beam units, which seem to give the car a slight bifocal appearance.

On the coachwork side there have been quite a few modifications and improvements. The interior, at both front and rear, has been re-upholstered, the woodwork repolished and in the rear compartment the vanity-sets in the quarter lights were removed. In 1969 it was decided to replace the seven valve radio set with a transistor MW and LW set and the opportunity was taken to place the radio in the rearwards-facing position, as on the Phantom Vs.

One of the persistent problems with the Phantom IV and its sister car, 4 BP 5, has been water leakage into the rear compartment through the glass section of the roof. About 120 screws had to be removed and a more waterproof type of felt fitted into place.

Prince Charles, who uses the car quite frequently, was surprised on one occasion to see steam issuing from the rear compartment heater outlet. This was traced to a leaking hose. Work on the aluminium bodywork, especially the running boards and sills, was an expensive refurbishment costing nearly £3,500. However, chassis repairs have been non-existent, probably because of the efficient central chassis lubrication system. It does though spew a little oil on to the outside of the chassis when pumped vigorously by the chauffeur. As one anonymous Rolls-Royce engineer observed, 'Rolls-Royce are not very well house trained!'

In 1985 with the two Phantom IVs' mileage collectively reaching well over a quarter of a million miles, it became imperative to look closely at the practicality of keeping both cars roadworthy for constant use. Rolls-Royce were keen to retire both cars and replace with vehicles which they felt were more representative of their current range.

The supply of spares for a model which had seen but sixteen purchased examples was acute. The following year this was brought home when the limousine (4 AF 2) blew a headgasket the night before the Royal Wedding of the Duke of York. No spare could be located in time and hurriedly the London demonstrator Phantom VI was pressed into service to accompany the Hooper Landaulette in carrying the bridesmaids and pages to Westminster Abbey.

Almost ten years previously, Rolls-Royce had estimated that to return both Phantom IVs to pristine condition would cost around £25,000 per car: inflation by the mid to late '80s would have made the figure horrific. Despite the fact that the Hooper car was younger and had covered less mileage it was decided that it should be retired first; although it is still owned by the Queen and kept at Sandringham. Being a landaulette it had from time to time to have the head leather renewed and the skills and cost of doing this every so often, coupled with the inevitable replacing of the ash framework in that area, probably swung the decision. So the first Phantom IV soldiers on, albeit in the main in the Greater London area. It is said to be the favourite of Prince Charles and if that is the case it is assured a future.

5

THE QUEEN'S FIRST PHANTOM

'JUBILEE'
Phantom IV Chassis 4 BP 5

WITH ONE CUCKOO (Phantom I V 4 A F 2) in the Daimler nest at the Royal Mews at Buckingham Palace following the accession of Queen Elizabeth I I, Rolls-Royce were hardly going to let an opportunity slip away. Though the Daimler Straight Eights transferred to her after the King's death were relatively youthful – one under three years old and the others under five – Rolls-Royce decided to act. Across at Daimler there was equal concern. The Coventry firm had seen the Queen's Phantom I V take precedence on most major engagements involving the State cars, with the Daimlers trailing behind, carrying Her Majesty's attendants.

What happened next was a moderate outlay by Rolls-Royce and a great deal of consternation on the part of the motor manufacturers who had been suppliers of State motor carriages for the best part of half a century. With commendable anticipation, Rolls-Royce diverted a Phantom I V chassis, planned to be bodied with four-door cabriolet coachwork, to Hooper & Co. Even before the Coronation had taken place Rolls-Royce decided to go ahead with a ceremonial car and where better to build a State car than the traditional coachbuilders Hoopers? Ironically the Hooper Company had been acquired by the Birmingham Small Arms company during the Second World War and B S A also owned Daimler! The move by Rolls-Royce was seen to be a real threat to Daimler's Royal monopoly.

The decision to body Phantom I V chassis 4 B P 5 with a State landaulette design was made on February 17, 1953. As there was no immediate hurry for the new car, the chassis did not reach the Western Avenue works of Hoopers until November 9. In the middle of June, however, a code name was chosen for the new car; it was to be called 'Jubilee', presumably for the reason that the following year, 1954, would be the Golden Jubilee of Rolls-Royce's foundation.

Quite by coincidence the Crown Agents for the Colonies had also ordered a new ceremonial car for the Governor of Singapore. This too was a State Landaulette and both cars were built in parallel. The Governor's Silver Wraith chassis No. BLW 92 was delivered to Hoopers on the same day as 'Jubilee' and quite curiously was off test just a day later than the other new Rolls-Royce ceremonial car. Apart from the chassis lengths both cars are remarkably similar. (The author now has in his guardianship the Singapore car.)

Meanwhile, Hoopers' chief designer (also a director of the company), Osmond Rivers, set to work on the design of the ceremonial car. He was instructed that all the internal dimensions were to be exactly as those on the Daimler Straight Eights. Chassis 4 BP 5 arrived at Hoopers with an automatic gearbox, the first time it had been put in a Phantom IV as an original fitment. It was also supplied with a full-flow oil filter which had been successfully introduced in the current Rolls-Royce models late in 1951. Phantom IVs up to February 1953 had had the old bypass filter in their specification. But this was only the start of a specification that Rolls-Royce wanted to make as comprehensive as possible, a car that would convince the Queen's advisers to buy Rolls-Royce.

As it was envisaged that the car would probably travel abroad a great deal, much thought was given to the heating and ventilation. At the time of the Phantom's construction the Queen's new yacht *Britannia* was nearing completion and the length and the width of the Royal car was checked against the garage built on the yacht.

The new Phantom, like the Daimlers at the Palace, was built with a manual folding black leather landaulette head, complete with a heavy lining reinforced for soundproofing with black horsehair. Just forward of this, but still ahead of the electric division, was a Triplex glass section which

This 1954 Silver Wraith (chassis B L W 92) was made for the Governor of Singapore. In 1959 it conveyed H R H Prince Philip on a visit to the 'Lion' city. Now back in Europe this car has been used by the Royal family during their visits to British forces on the Continent.

could be covered at will by an electrically-driven metal blind. The windows, likewise, could be operated at the touch of a switch and the power operation extended to the rear quarter lights (*i.e.* rear quarter windows) which had to be lowered when erecting the landaulette head to prevent the cant-rails fouling the frameless glass.

The radio for the rear compartment was set into the centre armrest and was the latest in technology from H M V; it had a chromium-plated control panel whilst the amplifier was in the boot and the aerial was fitted under the car with the twin speakers hidden behind the upholstery at either side of the back of the division. The front compartment had its own set which was of the type then in current use on the self-drive Rolls-Royce models, except that the aerial was an electric one and was fitted to the front offside wing.

There were two reading lights at waist level in the rear compartment

LEFT *A chauffeur's eye view of the dashboard of the State landaulette, chassis 4 BP 5. When it was built this car had the most comprehensive heating and ventilation system of any Rolls-Royce. The short lever in the quadrant behind the steering wheel is the selector lever for the automatic gearbox. On the floor below the steering column, the circular button is the foot-operated headlight dip-switch, whilst the chromium handle (lower right) is the handbrake lever.*

LEFT *The rear compartment of the State landaulette showing the spacious rear seat, flanked by the interior heating controls. All the side windows are power operated, even the rear quarter lights. Waist-level reading lights are concealed under small flaps in the walnut waist rail. The rectangular, polished wooden inserts in each armrest are pull-out ashtrays.*

whilst for special illumination at night there were two lights fitted high up on the back of the division and two more set into the roof just above the rear seats; these of course could be switched on by the chauffeur. A winding eight-day clock made by Smiths with a blue face and white hands and numerals was situated facing rearwards at the centre top of the division.

The car was furnished with navy blue cloth and carpet to the front compartment and in the rear, grey West of England cloth was used with a matching mohair rug; the boot was fitted with a black trimmed carpet. The woodwork of both compartments was in a light burr walnut. The scheme was exactly as on the later Daimler Straight Eights. The car was painted with a black roof and wings, whilst elsewhere Royal Claret was used, this being extended to the window frames where they were unchromed.

Finally, 4 B P 5 was the first car to be fitted with the new-style heraldic shield. In 1954 Lucas came up with a modified illumination scheme for the roof-mounted shields. Previously this had been a rather cumbersome system with external lighting shining on to the shield at night. Now Lucas contrived a system whereby the shield, when placed in the roof socket, made contact with two copper strips which carried power to the lighting built into the shield itself. The shield was made up from Perspex and the Royal Arms were emblazoned on to the front exterior.

This proved so successful that existing cars in the State Fleet were slowly converted to the new system. However, it was still possible for the old-style shields to be used should the new ones not be available. The new shields proved expensive and even today the only illuminated shields are those of H M The Queen and the Queen Mother. Although 4 B P 5 was not built to Royal Command it was nonetheless fitted with a small blue police light at the front of the windscreen. Thus, on April 29, 1954, the Rolls-Royce challenge to Daimler was completed.

Through their holding company B S A, Daimler were fully aware of the progress of the new Phantom I V and the threat the vehicle represented to their holding the Royal Warrant. The reason for their lack of immediate response was quite simply that they did not have a new chassis upon which to display their product. The Straight Eight had been discontinued and the new D K 400 was not to be exhibited until the forthcoming Earls Court

Motor Show, some six months after the new Rolls-Royce had been licensed. Also, the DK 400 chassis was as yet untried and, indeed, at the Motor Show the first example on show differed both mechanically and chassis-wise from what was to follow.

Immediately after the 1954 Earls Court Show, BSA chairman Sir Bernard Docker was understandably keen to build a competitor to the Phantom IV. His reply was to order the construction of two vehicles, a State landaulette and a State limousine, both on the untried chassis. These were to take almost two years to complete, and in retrospect that was fatal. Although every effort had been made to improve on the Straight Eight chassis, the DK 400 was a bitter disappointment. It handled badly, produced tremors through the coachwork and it lacked automatic transmission; these shortcomings, along with the very heavy steering, did not endear it to potential customers. The coachwork on the 10 ft 10 in chassis was much lighter, more sleek with built-in headlights, and the glass area to the rear compartment was an improvement. But with such a relatively short wheelbase there could not be an imposing bonnet and this was one area where the Phantom IV scored heavily.

Whereas the coachwork on the Daimler DK 400 State limousine from the scuttle rearwards looked very similar to the H. J. Mulliner Phantom IV in the Royal Mews, the DK 400 State landaulette was an exact copy of the Phantom IV from the same position rearwards. There was one major improvement over the Rolls-Royce, which concerned the lowering and raising of the hood on the Daimler landaulette. It was an entirely automatic operation and considering that this was in the days before micro-relays it was an extremely sophisticated operation and therefore worth describing in some detail.

At the front of the rear offside armrest was a switch which, when depressed, undid two locks in the roof of the car; this released the landaulette head, which then folded back. To raise the head the technology was more complex. When the switch was held down, the rear quarter-light glasses first dropped to avoid fouling the cant-rails, then the head lifted, and touched a micro-switch at the side of the fixed portion of the roof. This then activated two revolving snail locks, which curled out and pulled the head down tight;

at the end of their travel they hit another micro-switch, which then completed the circuit and turned the power off. This whole operation lasted about 45 seconds and must have fascinated the Royal Household who were impressed enough to have the 1949 Daimler Straight Eight (chassis 51740) converted to the system. Incidentally, to prevent The Queen from lowering the head by accident whilst on the move the switch in the rear compartment could only be operated when an override switch was pulled out on the front dashboard.

Whilst Daimler, through Hoopers, were busying themselves with their new cars, Rolls-Royce set about courting the Crown Equerry, Brigadier Walter Sale, and, of course, the new Monarch. It was intimated that the new Phantom IV would be held in readiness for Her Majesty's exclusive use and for that reason the car was garaged at Hythe Road, the London depot for Rolls-Royce. As the vehicle was not actually owned by The Queen it had to be registered; at first it was given a Cheshire numberplate STU 763 but later this was changed to OXR 2. Because of the work the management had in mind for the Phantom IV landaulette, the number plates could be easily detached and were secured by wing nuts. The front plate was easily undone but the rear was specially made up by a company called Cornercroft Engineering Ltd, who provided an internally illuminated plate which was fixed above the rear bumper, When the car was required for Royal use it was simply a matter of unscrewing the plates and disconnecting the power feed to the rear plate from the rear junction box, just behind the plate itself.

The car began to make intermittent appearances at Royal events and an early triumph came a year after its completion at the opening of the 1955 session of Parliament. It was to be the first time that the carriage drive was cancelled, because of a nationwide rail strike. For some reason, the Mulliner Phantom IV was not available (it was around this time that this car was fitted with an automatic gearbox). Anyway, a call to Hythe Road by the Crown Equerry early on the particular morning brought the new car around to the Royal Mews. There the plates were removed and the shield and Royal Standard mounted on the roof. Luckily, Rolls-Royce had been able to get permission from the Crown Equerry and the Queen's private secretary to have the heraldic painter G. C. Francis add his skills to the car

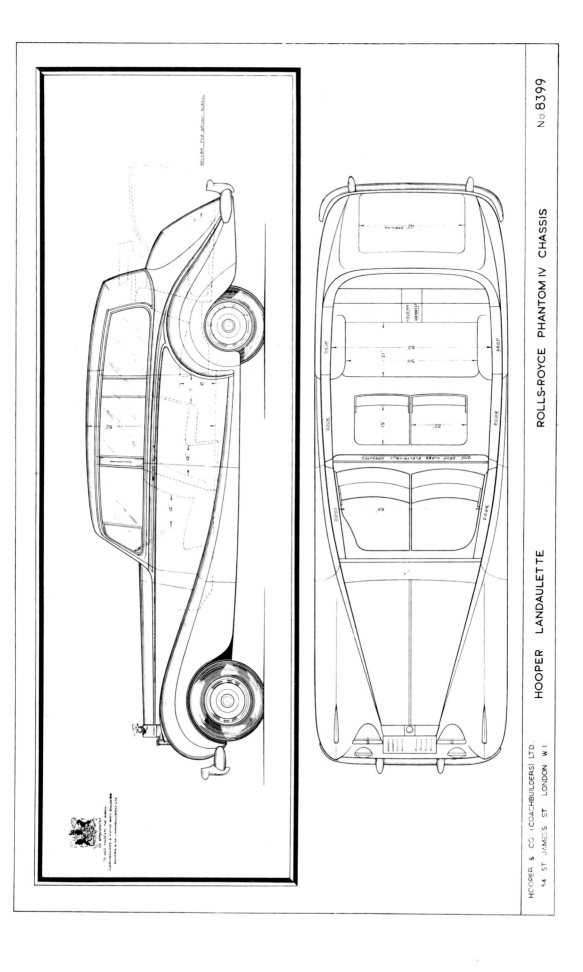

HOOPER & CO (COACHBUILDERS) LTD.   HOOPER LANDAULETTE   ROLLS-ROYCE PHANTOM IV CHASSIS

54 ST JAMES'S ST LONDON W.I.

No. 8399

LEFT *Original coachbuilder's drawing for the landaulette,
indicating the electrically operated division; and (*ABOVE*) the
finished car ready for delivery. At this stage it was fitted with the
latest pattern of bumpers. These were later changed to match
those of the older Phantom IV.*

earlier in the year. He had painted Her Majesty's Royal Crest, encircled by the collar of the Order of The Garter and surmounted by the Royal Crown, on the rear doors and the boot lid.

Off to open her first Parliament in the pouring June rain went Her Majesty. Daimler must have been particularly chagrined to see in the newspapers the next day a photograph showing The Queen in the Rolls-

This Daimler D K 400 State landaulette was originally expected to enter Royal service. The bodywork by Hooper was virtually identical to that on the Rolls-Royce Phantom I V which did become part of the Royal fleet. Thirty years later, when owned by the Author, it was again put to Royal use during a visit to the Royal Artillery in West Germany, escort provided by The King's Troop of the Royal Horse Artillery.

Royce landaulatte sweeping out of Palace Yard after the State opening, while two of her official State Daimlers hovered in the background, ready to convey those waiting upon Her.

Bigger things were in store. As the New Year approached, preparations were well in hand for The Queen's visit to West Africa. The Colonial administration in Nigeria had approached Rolls-Royce for a ceremonial car and in the event it turned out to be a monopoly for the company. Three Silver Wraiths belonging to various Provincial Governors were used, as well as two brand-new Silver Clouds, which had been introduced at the last London Motor Show and were shipped out along with the Phantom IV State landaulette. Because of the intense heat experienced in the tropics, the radiators of the new arrivals were modified with fan cowlings. As the major engagements were to be undertaken with 4 BP 5, that car received a number of extra refinements.

A set of loose covers was made up for the car, two miniature fans were placed high up in the corners of the rear compartment, either side of the division, and two extra interior lights were fitted to the rear folding hoopstick (these lights were to be removed on the car's return to the UK). All the cars were in place by the time Her Majesty arrived on January 28, 1956, the landaulette having left the UK on December 8, 1955.

Rolls-Royce, of course, were keen to see that everything went off as well as could be arranged. It was The Queen's first major tour since her visit to Australia and New Zealand a little under two years earlier, and Daimler had had the lion's share of the publicity out of that event. The Governments of both Dominions at the time had at last been able to make use of a whole fleet of Straight Eight Daimlers which had been shipped out in the late 1940s for King George VI's visit which, because of his illness, never took place. To ensure that any eventuality could be coped with, Rolls-Royce despatched two engineers to Nigeria; T. Johnson and W. Garner were there well before the Royal Party arrived and remained until the tour ended on February 16.

Reading the reports nearly three decades later, it is not difficult to capture the flavour of the period: the battles with dusty roads, enthusiastic African drivers, agitated ADC's and officialdom in the heat. Mr Garner received the Royal Victoria Medal for his contribution to the success of the

Tour and Mr Johnson the MVO. Presenting the RVM at 8.30 on the morning of her departure from Lagos, the Queen remarked how well everything had gone. However, there had been one or two near scrapes, like the time the Governor of Northern Nigeria's Silver Wraith had rolled to a halt with Her Majesty and the Duke on board. It then refused to start, but eventually responded to a push. The Rolls-Royce representative reported with some relief that the Queen and the Duke played up the situation and treated the whole affair as a huge joke. However, London requested an immediate explanation and this reported that the car had been idling for at least half an hour in the hot sun and that had caused the problem.

This had happened on February 3 at Kaduna and in his report Mr Johnson was at pains to explain that after a short time in the Nigerian sunshine the heat could make a car's bodywork too hot to touch. The situation was also complicated by the Governor's European driver changing the sparking plugs and the high-tension harness for a set intended for a Bedford truck. There had also been problems with batteries, and the petrol had had to be constantly filtered and strained; but 4 BP 5 sailed through the ordeal and in the next three years Hoopers received two orders from the Nigerian Government for two landaulettes, but on the much more prosaic Silver Wraith chassis. Undoubtedly it was the Nigeria Tour which won Rolls-Royce their spurs and for the Phantom IV a steady demand from the Palace for its services on other tours overseas.

The following year, 1957, saw the Phantom IV 4 BP 5 in the Channel Islands, France and Denmark. For the visit to the island of Guernsey the car was flown across by Silver City Airways. The Channel Islands visit was

With the head raised (Inset) *the Phantom IV State landaulette is seen here in a somewhat gloomy Royal Mews, just prior to its debut at the State opening of Parliament. The planned State drive was cancelled owing to a railway strike. This car was used instead of the Mulliner limousine which was away having a new gearbox fitted. Later in the day* (MAIN PICTURE) *the rain abated. Rolls-Royce Ltd had a photographer on hand to record how the car looked with its head folded down.*

interesting because whilst the Phantom was on Guernsey the virtually matching Daimler DK 400 landaulette was undertaking one of its first major engagements on Jersey; it may well have been that the Crown Equerry, Brigadier Walter Sale, was trying the cars out almost side-by-side. However, only Rolls-Royce carried the heraldry on the rear doors and the boot lid. Upon its return from the Channel Islands the Phantom IV was hurriedly despatched to the north-west for a Royal tour of Cheshire.

The other two foreign tours that year, to France and Denmark, put the seal on the Royal use of the State landaulette. Lady Docker once remarked that whilst holidaying in France she had had to remind admiring onlookers on more than one occasion that it was not a Delahaye she was driving but a Daimler. The very diffidence of Daimler, with only a 'D' emblem on the hubcaps, may well have contributed to their lack of public impact. In contrast, the vision of that unmistakable Rolls-Royce radiator and the Spirit of Ecstasy atop it, left onlookers in no doubt that they were in the presence of automotive greatness. Certainly the French were left in no doubt: the Rolls-Royce undertook all the Royal engagements when the Queen was not accompanied by the French President.

The most crucial accolade was probably the State Visit to Denmark which took place earlier in the year, May 18–25. Once again Rolls-Royce were asked to loan the Phantom IV and, if this were possible, for the car to be embarked a few days earlier on board the Royal Yacht *Britannia* and returned to the United Kingdom the same way at the end of the tour. Without hesitation, as may be imagined, the company concurred. As before, an engineer accompanied the Royal Party and again it was the fortunate Mr Garner who undertook the task, this time also driving on occasions. At the conclusion of the visit the Queen sailed for Scotland with 'Jubilee' safely on board in the relatively minute garage. *Britannia* docked at Invergordon after the overnight journey and whilst the Royal Party disembarked, a lighter received the landaulette on to its deck for a quick passage to the jetty to await the Queen. The car motored to Balmoral and remained there until June 4 when one of the Royal chauffeurs returned it to Hythe Road.

At about this time, Jack Scott, the sales director at Rolls-Royce in Conduit Street, London, discussed with the Crown Equerry the possibility of constructing a four-door cabriolet for use on overseas tours. H. J. Mulliner prepared a sketch for submission to Jack Scott and suggested the use of power operation of the hood mechanism. 'It would be too awful if the car were used in the tropics and a sudden storm blew up, to have a platoon of flunkeys struggling to erect a top by hand, whils the dignatories occupying the car tried to look pleasant and unconscious of it all.' But by the time the drawing was made in the summer of 1957 for submission to the Royal Mews, there had been further developments in the replacement programme for the State cars and the project lapsed.

OVERLEAF *The similarity in the coachwork of the Rolls-Royce and the Daimler landaulettes can easily be seen if this picture is compared with that of the Daimler on page 78. The Phantom IV is shown at the Roodee in Chester. HM the Queen was there to present new colours to three battalions of the Cheshire Regiment.*

BELOW *Shipped out to West Africa in 1956, the Phantom IV landaulette did sterling work for the image of Rolls-Royce in the major cities of Nigeria. This picture shows how splendidly suited to such occasions is the landaulette with the head folded down. It was so hot on this trip that cooling fans were fitted above the division in order to provide an air flow for the rear seat occupants. The fans remain in the car to this day.*

ABOVE *Just prior to its handover to the Royal Mews in January 1959, the Phantom IV was completely checked over at the London Service Depot of Rolls-Royce Ltd, then in Hythe Road. Note the elegance of the rear of the car – an aspect that so often seems to be forgotten by some stylists. The overriders have been changed so as to match those of the earlier car.*

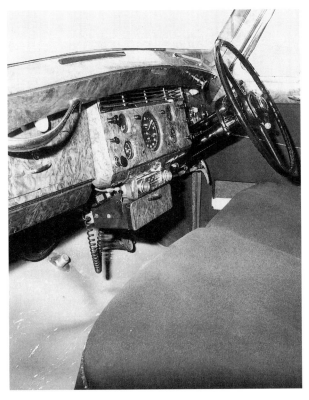

ABOVE *By the early 1980s the front compartment had acquired a radio telephone. It was concealed behind a polished wooden panel immediately below the normal radio. Rather more prosaically, the front floor is covered in linoleum – an indication of the considerable amount of wear to which these cars are subjected.*

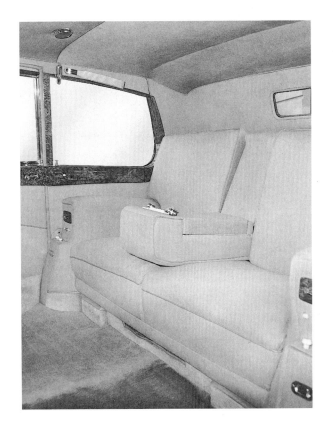

LEFT *Taken at the same time as the picture of the front compartment, the rear looks little different to when the car was first commissioned. There are though, some subtle changes: a new transistor radio has displaced the earlier valve set in the centre armrest, whilst behind that, a radio telephone has been fitted in place of the concealed mirror. The seat has been re-upholstered and the cushion divided. Illustrations on page 72 show how it originally appeared.*

It was this State car renewal programme that eventually led to Phantom IV 4 BP 5 being purchased by the Palace. Rolls-Royce, as promised, had kept the State landaulette exclusively for the use of the Royal Family, and the Queen in particular. When the decision to switch to Rolls-Royce was mooted in late 1957 the company thought that a deal involving the Phantom IV and the two new Silver Phantom Vs (as they were originally termed) could be concluded. The Royal Family insisted that the new cars should be purchased on purely commercial terms and were very strongly against any suggestion of favoured treatment. But the possibility of 'Jubilee' in the arrangement meant that Rolls-Royce could absorb some of the cost themselves in disposing of what was in effect a used car; by this time its mileage was nearing 10,000.

On November 4, 1958 the Crown Equerry wrote to Conduit Street to confirm the agreement of the Palace financial advisers that 'Jubilee' should be acquired, and it was to be delivered to the Royal Mews on January 30, ready to meet Her Majesty on her return from Sandringham. A slight quandary faced Rolls-Royce at this time when the Crown Agents in London on behalf of the Government of Ghana approached the company to loan the landaulette for the forthcoming tour of that country. Not wishing to breach a confidence, Rolls-Royce delayed making a reply, but did intimate that they would loan a suitable car and organize a driver and that a representative would be in attendance.

On January 22, 1959, a week before the handover, the sales department at Rolls-Royce sent a letter to A. G. Firman, one of the directors of Hooper & Co. It must have sent a shiver up the backs of the Daimler management, who through their subsidiary heard about the contents in no time at all: 'Her Majesty The Queen has decided to take over "Jubilee" as one of her official cars.'

With the arrival of the second Phantom, the oldest 1947 Daimler Straight Eight was sent to Stratstone, the main Daimler Distributors in London, for disposal; they had looked after the Royal Family in motoring matters for some 55 years. Stratstone tried to sell the car to the Middlesex County Council but the Council considered the price too high for a car then 12 years old. In the end the Council acquired the DK 400 State Landaulette for £4,950 being offered £600 for a trade-in on their old vehicle. Up to this time the car on which Daimler had staked so much had travelled a mere 4,977 miles in service for the Royal Family as a stand-in car. The sister State limousine had already been sold by this time to the Chairman of the Cementation group of companies, having completed about double the landaulette's mileage in Royal usage. The Rolls-Royce challenge to the Daimler supremacy was all but complete.

In the week that Hooper's had been told of the 'Jubilee' acquisition, a delighted Conduit Street official wrote an instruction to Hythe Road, 'In the boot of "Jubilee" are the original number-plates and the licence disc; these are now completely redundant as the car will become a State Vehicle. Please forward the licence disc to W J, who will arrange cancellation. The number-plates can be scrapped.'

Since its acquisition over thirty years ago this Phantom I V has until very recently been in constant use. (When the Phantom Vs arrived with their air-conditioning for hot climates, they were naturally preferred for overseas tours.) Not surprisingly for such a long and active life, there are many anecdotes about 'Jubilee'. The car was, for example, used by Princess Margaret after her wedding in 1960. The car drove the couple to Tower Pier to embark on the Royal Yacht, but the crush of onlookers was so great that the landaulette was forced to slow to a crawl and the police had to link arms to let the Phantom I V proceed through the melee. Later it was discovered that there were three or four parallel lines down each side of the car scratched quite deeply into the Royal Claret paintwork. Later these were traced to the buttons on the uniforms of the police who had been pressed hard up against the car by the happy throng of onlookers.

Up until its retirement the car had covered close to 130,000 miles. There have been few external changes to the car. To bring it into line with the earlier Mulliner Phantom I V the bumpers and over-riders were changed to the earlier flat type. In 1969 a new transistor radio was installed, the old-type underfloor antenna was done away with and an electric wing aerial to match that on the offside was fitted. The car was repainted from time to time and the chrome similarly rejuvenated.

One feature that has required replacement is the leather landaulette head. This was last done in 1981, when Mulliner Park Ward undertook the task with their craftsmen Ray Farley and Eugene O'Sullivan spending many weeks unstitching the cloth lining for cleaning and rebuilding the hoopsticks where necessary with ash framing. Later Connolly black hammered leather was stitched into place, the whole operation costing about £2,000. The car looked particularly smart and no longer leaked. Sadly, it seems that the only time the head was lowered was during the State Drive when the Court was in residence at Holyrood House in Edinburgh. The Scottish Sword of State was to be carried in the procession and this massive item would have penetrated the roof if the head of the car had not been dropped.

Until its retirement to the Sandringham motor museum the Hooper landaulette was covering about 3,000 miles a year. It seemed to find favour with the Prince and Princess of Wales in its latter active years and they also found the old Mulliner to their liking. They are both extremely easy cars from which to alight and were therefore suitable for evening engagements

After 30 years of service, some of it as far afield as West Africa, the Hooper-bodied Phantom IV landaulette is now in effect retired at Sandringham. It was loaned for display at the 1987 Essen Motor Show. It could, of course, be restored and returned to Royal Duty along with Her Majesty's other Phantom IV, should the need arise. (As a point of interest, the Spanish Royal family now use the Phantom IVs that originally belonged to General Franco.)

when the Princess had to leave a car as elegantly as possible. As regards the Hooper car, it had been thought by the Palace that after the delivery of the Phantom Vs then Rolls-Royce might buy the two older cars back. This was not pursued, although the company had said that they would have little difficulty finding a ready market for both cars. One close shave for the landaulette came in the winter of 1967 when the agile mind of Prince Philip thought that it might be an idea to prolong the car's usefulness by having it converted to a shooting brake. Rolls-Royce were rather reluctant to accept the challenge at a time when they had committed a lot of designers and drawing office staff to the new Silver Shadow range and its subsequent derivatives. The then fairly new Crown Equerry Col. John Miller M C, was equally enthusiastic; and to galvanize Rolls-Royce into action mentioned that the St Cuthbert's Cooperative Society in Edinburgh had just done some excellent work on the Scottish State Coach. Rolls-Royce saw the option and encouraged the line with this Edinburgh-based company. Although they had tackled the coach with a new top and enlarged the windows, they became rather cautious about taking on a motor car with road stresses with which they were unfamiliar. Strangely, Prince Philip then took over the car as his own for a number of years, probably reconciling himself to the fact that such a high-roofed shooting brake was not terribly practical after all.

In the autumn of 1987, following the delivery of Her Majesty's latest Phantom V I the landaulette was withdrawn from regular usage. Unlike the old Daimlers at Sandringham where it is now housed, the car is insured for road use and will from time to time be pressed into service. Having travelled to the continent of Africa, around Europe and over the length and breadth of Britain it is good to know that the car can still come out of retirement. It had the distinction of being the last Hooper-bodied motor vehicle in the Royal Mews; now it joins the first one, a Daimler, built in the reign of Queen Victoria over ninety years ago. Quite curiously, it did make one more journey to Europe before leaving for Sandringham. In December 1987 the car travelled to the Essen Motor Show to feature as an exhibit; a unique gesture from the Queen. But for once it travelled hidden from view, in a container.

6

A BRACE OF PHANTOMS FOR THE QUEEN

THE 'CANBERRA CARS'
Phantom Vs Chassis numbers: 5 AS 33 and 5 A T 34

THE IMPACT OF THE 1956 ROYAL TOUR OF NIGERIA no doubt played a major part in the shift from Daimler to Rolls-Royce. Later that year an intimation was given to Conduit Street that submissions to the Palace about car replacement might be met with a favourable response. The Duke of Edinburgh, like his Crown Equerry, Brigadier Walter Sale, favoured an all Rolls-Royce fleet at the Royal Mews but steps to re-equip could not be carried out overnight. Up to that time Daimler had served the Monarchy faithfully for well over half a century and Hooper & Co had been holders of the Royal Warrant since 1830. Besides, none of the three Daimlers in the Royal Mews was even 10 years old.

Rolls-Royce were keen to encourage the idea of a change and went to some lengths to show their enthusiasm for the project. In the summer of 1956 the Company had just missed supplying an open-top Bentley Continental for the Duke of Edinburgh's visit to Australia to open the Commonwealth Games. The scheme had foundered on import quotas which the Australian Government was rigidly observing at the time. Rolls-Royce felt that to ship out the car for a couple of days' work and then bring it back around the globe was not really viable. In the end, a Humber cabriolet which had been built for the 1949 Royal tour of the Antipodes was used. This car was ordered for the visit of King George VI but the monarch's illness had cancelled the tour.

Meanwhile the Phantom IV Landaulette was an almost permanent feature at the Royal Mews. By the end of March 1957 the Crown Equerry, at the request of the Queen's Deputy Treasurer, provided information regarding the cars in the Royal Mews. A plan was in preparation to bring the fleet up to date.

On March 21, 1958, the Rolls-Royce board were informed in strictest confidence that, following a meeting with the Crown Equerry, estimates would be submitted to Her Majesty's advisers to re-equip the State limousine fleet and that, providing all negotiations went satisfactorily, the replacement vehicles would be Rolls-Royce.

The man who liaised between the company and the Palace was Jack Scott, Rolls-Royce's Conduit Street senior sales director. He hoped that two cars would be ordered and hoped too that the Phantom IV landaulette could be included in the deal. At this point the company were asked to submit approximate prices three months hence.

It was envisaged that the in-house coachbuilders Park Ward would

build the coachwork for the chassis. Their last Royal order had been in 1939 on a Wraith for the Duke of Connaught. The Crown Equerry sought assurances that this concern would produce workmanship comparable to that of H. J. Mulliner and Hooper who had given every satisfaction in the past. The managing director of Park Ward, Charles Ward, and his designer Dick Robbins proceeded cautiously with a design. At the end of the three month period Rolls-Royce presented the financial figures to the Crown Equerry for discussion with the advisers to Her Majesty.

At about this time Rolls-Royce issued the first details of their new chassis to be introduced at the 1959 Earls Court Motor Show. They revealed to the Palace that the Phantom V would have a new V8 engine, power steering as standard and full air-conditioning. In the following 12 months the only specification change on the chassis-side was to alter the tyre size from 9.50×14 to 8.90×15. As well as the financial details and the chassis description, Brigadier Walter Sale received a colour drawing that revealed a revolutionary body to complement the car's running gear.

The Crown Equerry was assured that the interior dimensions would be almost identical to those of the Phantom IV. What was revolutionary was the Perspex dome for the rear compartment which made it light, airy and with good visibility whilst at the same time protecting the occupants from the elements.

Mr Peter Wharton of Park Ward made this splendid line drawing of the proposed body style which was submitted to the Crown Equerry at the Palace. One minor later change was that the Royal Standard was given its own trap-door in the roof, just behind the heraldic shield.

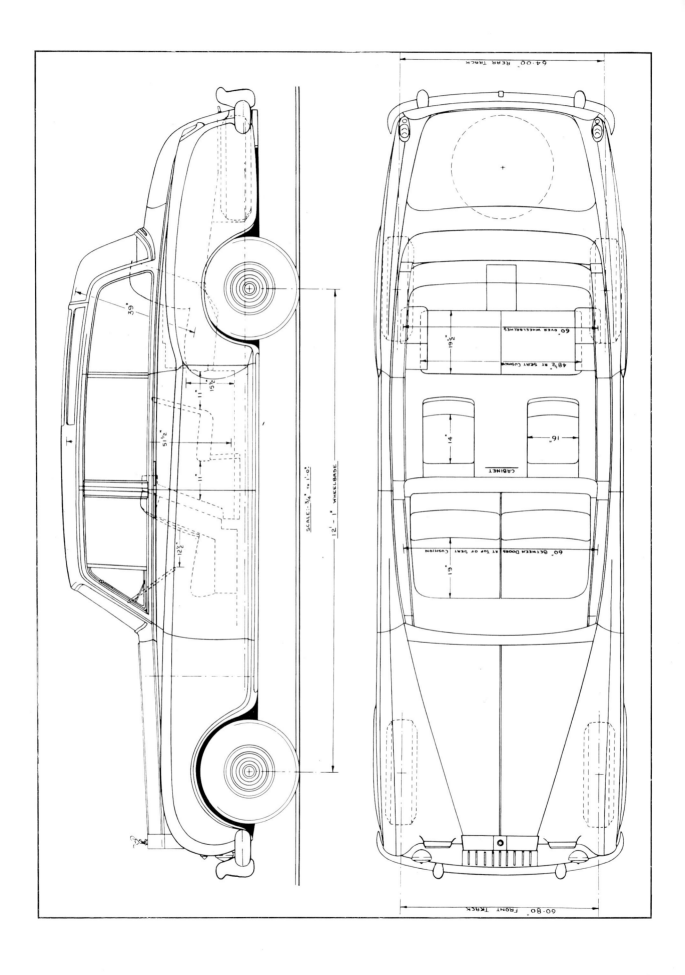

SCALE - ¾" TO 1'-0"

12'-1" WHEELBASE

39"

15½"

51½"

11"

12½"

64.00" REAR TRACK

60" OVER WHEELARCHES

19½"

48½" AT SEAT CUSHION

CABINET

14"

16"

60" BETWEEN DOORS AT TOP OF SEAT CUSHION

19"

60.80" FRONT TRACK

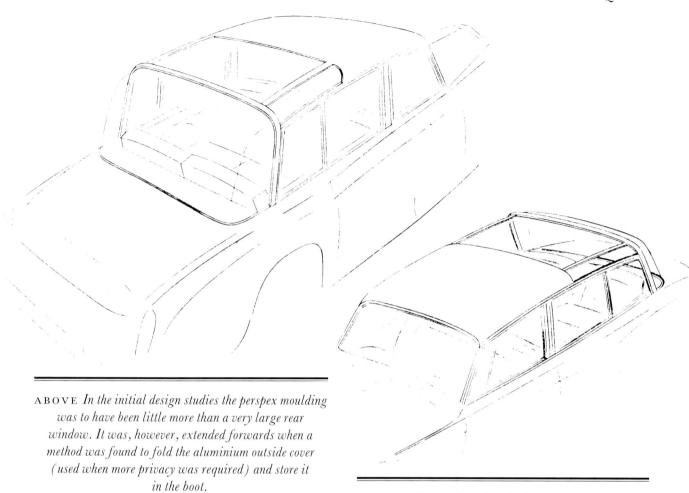

ABOVE *In the initial design studies the perspex moulding was to have been little more than a very large rear window. It was, however, extended forwards when a method was found to fold the aluminium outside cover (used when more privacy was required) and store it in the boot.*

OPPOSITE *Park Ward line drawing of the 1960 Phantom V.*

BELOW *Just to show that the Canberra domes weren't entirely revolutionary; Daimler had experimented with something similar in the 1950s.*

In mid-September Brigadier Sale spoke to Her Majesty on the subject and The Queen said that she would be discussing the matter very shortly with Prince Philip. Eight weeks elapsed before Rolls-Royce learned that they had the opportunity to wrest the coveted Royal Warrant from Daimler. The Palace had agreed to the purchase of two new Phantom Vs and would acquire the 'Jubilee' Phantom IV which was to be handed over to the Palace at the beginning of 1959. Jubilation reigned at Rolls-Royce and Park Ward, but it was discreetly expressed, following the Palace request that the matter be treated confidentially until an announcement to the Press on the delivery of the first car; and this was still 21 months away.

The designs of Park Ward for the new cars had obviously made a great impression on Prince Philip and he showed as much interest in the new vehicles as he had in his first Rolls-Royce delivered nearly 10 years previously. He asked that one or two changes be made to the design: including modification of the cant-rail to prevent it snagging the occupants' heads (or hats) when alighting; a suggestion that the air conditioning switches be easier to understand and be identifiable in the dark; and finally – a reminder of what it must be like to be constantly in the public eye – he asked if the division glass could be rather less curved as he sometimes used it as a looking glass, adding that it was often difficult to use a hand mirror in public... Inspector Perkins, Her Majesty's private detective, was also consulted as to whether the mounting and dismounting of the Royal shield and standard could be made any easier.

All this time there was a great risk of details of the new cars leaking out and so Park Ward at Willesden hit on the idea of telling their employees that the ceremonial cars were being prepared for use in Australia. Hence both vehicles were code-named, 'Canberra'. By a strange coincidence two cars were being prepared for Australia, not by Park Ward but by Hooper. It is sad to record that the two cabriolets they were preparing were the last they built for the use of the Royal Family. Within the year Hooper had ceased traditional coachbuilding on chassis provided by manufacturers.

One of the biggest problems that Park Ward had to wrestle with concerned the length of the Phantom V chassis. It was 19 ft 10 ins long, which was too lengthy to fit into the necessarily compact garage on board

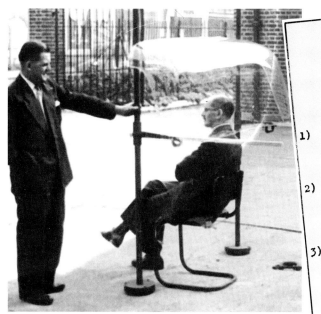

ABOVE *Passers-by glancing into the yard of Park Ward's works in High Road, Willesden, must have been curious at the sight of men posing under a large inverted goldfish bowl. In fact, members of the design team were conducting tests on the perspex rear section to assess its freedom from distortion.*

RIGHT *In the later stages of body-finishing, several points had to be cleared with the Palace.*

CANBERRA – Fittings under Query

1) A.A. and R.A.C. Badges – These appear to be special ones; are they changed from car to car should the older car not be used, or are new ones obtained?

2) Radiator mascot – We believe that on the H.J.M. car a 'George and Dragon' mascot was fitted but have seen the Rolls-Royce 'Lady' on the Hooper car. Which type will be fitted to Canberra?

3) Illuminated shield – The spigot at the base of the shield makes it interchangeable with other cars. Will a new shield be supplied for this car or will the previous ones be used? If so, we would appreciate having it on loan to be able to make sure that it fits snugly into our bayonet fitting on the roof.

4) Flag and post – Are these to be supplied with the car or are they interchangeable from another car?

5) St. Christopher Badge – Is one to be fitted on to the instrument board? We noticed that one was fitted on the H.J.M. car.

6) Is the interior trim to be grey as on the previous car?

RIGHT *Shortly before the Phantom was delivered, members of the press were invited to inspect what was a new and quite revolutionary Royal car.*

HMY *Britannia*. Although approximately 20 feet in length, the garage left no room for manoeuvring around the car. Eventually a solution was found. Designer Dick Robbins came up with the idea of de-mountable front and rear bumpers. This saved 9 inches and another $2\frac{1}{2}$ inches were saved by reducing the width of the apron between the bumpers and the bodywork at both ends of the car.

A lot of effort went into obtaining a distortion-free Perspex dome; many types and designs were tested until the right compromise was reached.

By May 1959 all major points had been finalized and the delivery date for the first Phantom V, chassis 5 AS 33, to Park Ward was set for the last week of August 1959. The other chassis, 5 AT 34, would follow later. By the last week of October Prince Philip made a secret visit to Park Ward to see for himself how the car was progressing. He tried the seating arrangements and also viewed the fitted dome-cover and how the cover to the Perspex dome could be stowed in the boot. A month later the coachbuilders had advanced to the stage where a number of queries concerning detail fitments to the car were referred to the Crown Equerry. These concerned the AA and RAC badges on the front apron, the special George and Dragon mascot for the radiator cap, the fitting of the illuminated heraldic shield to the roof and its electrical contacts and the Royal Standard arrangement behind the shield

PREVIOUS PAGE *The new Royal Phantom about to be delivered. It was very different to any other Royal car, particularly in the excellent view it afforded of the occupants.*

RIGHT *Not surprisingly, visibility from within was also excellent. The interior appeared light, airy and business-like. Again, the wide centre arm-rest was put to good use; it housed the air conditioning controls and the radio, plus a small compartment for a mirror and the stowage of oddments. A close-up of some of the controls on the Queen's side of the car (Inset) shows the superb finish and workmanship of the interior.*

ABOVE *When necessary, the rear of the car could be made very private by means of the covers (usually kept out of sight in the boot) being placed over the dome.*

RIGHT *It would be difficult to find any angle from which visibility in or out was not excellent through the perspex.*

boss (this was to be as on Princess Margaret's Phantom IV and on the modified Phantom IV in the Royal Mews).

There was a great deal of discussion about paintwork and trim. As on the other Phantom IV, the trim was to be dark blue to the front compartment and grey to the rear. This last item caused a problem until H. J. Mulliner located a roll of suitable material and sent it over to Willesden. The cabinetwork was walnut curl veneer, cross-banded with French walnut, whilst the carpet to the rear compartment was a light grey curly wool-mohair.

Since the Royal cars from earliest times had the body in Royal Claret and the wheel covers and wings in black, a dilemma presented itself. The Park Ward design did not lend itself easily to such treatment – there was a swage line picking out the front and rear wheel arches but this was a continuous line. For this and other reasons it was decided to reverse previous practice and use black for above the waistline and Royal Claret for the rest of bodywork. The picking-out line remained vermillion.

By March 1960 a divisional board meeting of Rolls-Royce discussed the progress of the two cars. Two points were raised. One was the possibility of reducing the height of the second car by one inch; in the end this was abandoned. The other point concerned the width of the occasional seats. The board wanted to know why it was that the car was now fitted with standard width occasional seats, which were much narrower than the Phantom IV's. It was explained that wider seats would foul the centre divison cabinet when the seats were not in use and folded away. By now all was nearly complete and a letter from the Crown Equerry on April 28 requested that delivery of the first car should be made at 10 am, May 10.

However, there was one service that Park Ward were eager to acquire from the experts, Hooper & Co. Hoopers were to close the coachbuilding side of their operations and vacate their Western Avenue premises on December 31, 1959 and re-open as Hooper Motor Services the following day at Kimberley Road, Kilburn. In September 1959, Osmond Rivers, a director and the chief designer at Hoopers, was invited by Rolls-Royce to lunch at Park Ward. At that meeting it was decided that Park Ward (and thereby Rolls-Royce) would purchase from Hooper all the designs, casting patterns, royal shields, flagstaffs and small blue police lights for the use of the new suppliers to the Palace. Osmond Rivers also advised on matters relating to relationships with High Commissions and Embassies both at home and overseas and also with British Governors and their representatives in the Colonies and the Dominions.

Finally, it was arranged that a member of the Hooper staff who was familiar with all the various requiements would transfer to Park Ward. Thus, continuity was ensured and Park Ward could inform the Palace that they were *au fait* with all arrangements necessary to carry out the task ahead.

On May 3, 1960, representatives of *Autocar* and *Motor* magazines visited Park Ward to photograph and write up the new State car. Apart from the new engine, the air-conditioning and the striking new bodywork, the journalists were also intrigued by the radio, which, as before, was in the centre armrest to the rear with another set for the driver up front. Although there were two aerials it was so arranged that in the event of breakdown of the rear compartment set the front set could be switched through to the back of the car.

A week later, at the appointed time, Driver Reid from Conduit Street took the car from Willesden out into the early morning traffic and headed towards Victoria and the Royal Mews at the back of Buckingham Palace. There he was met by the head chauffeur, Mr Chivers, senior Mews staff and the Crown Equerry. Senior Rolls-Royce management was represented by Jack Scott, who had taken over much of the responsibility for the car's

Park Ward and Rolls-Royce were justifiably proud of the new State car, the first to be specially made for a reigning British Monarch. The press release, however, was suitably restrained in its tone. Jack Scott, the Head of Sales, Rolls-Royce Ltd, Conduit Street, (who held considerable responsibility in the matter), wrote the note (BELOW RIGHT) to Park Ward in the afternoon of the delivery to Her Majesty of Her new car: understated but warmly received.

ROLLS-ROYCE LIMITED

TELEGRAMS:
"ROLHEAD PICCY, LONDON"
TELEPHONE:
MAYFAIR 6201 (7 LINES)

14-15 CONDUIT STREET, LONDON. W.1

MOTOR CAR DIVISION

CODES USED
A.B.C. (5TH EDITION)· BENTLEYS
MARCONI · MOTOR TRADE
WESTERN UNION

OUR REF.

YOUR REF. <u>PRESS INFORMATION</u> for release 14.00 hrs. B.S.T. May 10th 1960.

<u>A NEW ROYAL CAR.</u>

A new Rolls-Royce Phantom V was delivered to Her Majesty, the Queen, today. The car is a standard Seven Passenger Limousine produced by Messrs. Park Ward & Co. Ltd., and similar to the model listed in the manufacturer's catalogue for universal use in both Home and Export markets – the Retail price being £6,600 plus Purchase Tax. The car is painted in the Royal colours: Maroon and Black and upholstered in Grey West of England cloth.

Modifications have been incorporated to the rear quarter windows and roof, which give exceptionally clear visibility from both inside and outside the car. The roof is fitted with a glass centre and Perspex side panels and the rear section of the roof is made in one piece of moulded Perspex. The interior of the car can be illuminated by fluorescent lighting when required. The centre roof glass can be covered from inside the car by an electrically-operated sliding panel. A folding metal exterior roof panel encloses the Perspex section at the rear when the car is not being used for ceremonial purposes, and is secured by locks with special safety escutcheons to prevent accidental opening. The ... stored in the luggage com...

Fresh, warm or refri... ducts from which the air ... is a feature on all Rolls-... as in the case of all Phan... door glasses are electrica... occasional seats are fitte...

The car has been suppl... and photographs are attache...

*

Sales to Park Ward
CW

JS.7/KEM 10/5/60

C: LS - for information

Canberra

You will be pleased to hear that Her Majesty the Queen was most satisfied with the new car which I delivered today. She spent some time in studying all the various fittings and accessories, even to asking questions regarding technical points on the new engine and chassis.

Her Majesty has asked me to convey to all employees of Park Ward who were responsible for the production of this car, her appreciation of the excellent workmanship both as regards appearance and comfort.

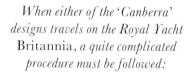

When either of the 'Canberra' designs travels on the Royal Yacht Britannia, *a quite complicated procedure must be followed:*

TOP, LEFT TO RIGHT
Remove front bumper, remove rear bumper, drive onto hoist and lift hoist onto barge.

FAR LEFT *The barge travels to H M Yacht*

LEFT *H M Yacht lifts the hoist aboard.*

BELOW LEFT *The car must now be slid sideways – a snug fit.*
BELOW *Bumpers restored before disembarkation.*

construction. Later the car was driven around to the quadrangle inside the Palace and the Queen spent some time studying the various fitments and the accessories and quizzed Jack Scott on several points about the new engine and the chassis. Her Majesty requested that her appreciation of the excellent workmanship, appearance and comfort of the car be conveyed to those who had worked for so long on the vehicle.

The coachbuilding time had been just under eight months. Meanwhile, the sister chassis was being completed and it was hoped that delivery would be in February 1961. Originally it had been intended to deliver six months after the first car but a few modifications were incorporated into 5 A T 34 and this delayed it joining 5 A S 33 in the Mews.

The first of the 'Canberras' settled down, but just two months after delivery an evening call from the Royal Mews had engineer John Rowe (who had been involved on Royal overseas tours) hot-footing it to the Palace. Both Mr Chivers and his deputy Harold Purvey reported an intermittent grating noise from the air conditioning plant. Eventually this was traced to a faulty compressor clutch. Subsequent units were modified to obviate the problem. As there were now three Rolls-Royces in the Mews and only one Daimler remaining (chassis 51172) emergency visits by the London service station of Rolls-Royce took over from Daimler.

Some of the idiosyncracies of the chauffeurs came to light. Senior Chauffeur Mr Chivers featured in a fair share of interesting stories. He was apparently very fond of golf: sometimes an urgent call would come through from the Royal Mews about a car being unserviceable, as often as not on a Friday afternoon. Engineers recall in one or two instances arriving in great haste at either Windsor or at the Mews, only to be told that the rear compartment clock was defective. The fact that it was a wind-up type and hadn't been touched for nearly eight days (the tension time of the spring) hadn't apparently crossed the mind of the chauffeur disappearing through the door with his golf bags . . . His car was unserviceable, thus the number two car and deputy chauffeur had been sent on Royal duties!

By November 1960 the last of the Daimlers had gone and in February the second Phantom V, chassis 5 A T 34 was delivered. Following previous practice, the latest car became the No.1 State car, with the first 'Canberra' relegated to No.2. The Phantom IV landaulette became No.3 and the H. J. Mulliner Phantom IV, No.4. From February 1960 until the delivery of the new Phantom VI in April 1978 these four cars were to be the sole State transport for the Royal Family in the United Kingdom and on many tours overseas.

After the delivery of chassis 5 AT 34, the opportunity was taken to carry out routine maintenance on 5 AS 33 at Hythe Road, Rolls-Royce's London service station. Since the introduction of the V8 engine in autumn 1959 on all Rolls-Royce models, a few minor reliability problems had come to light. So while the car was at Hythe Road, certain items were replaced – springs, valves and other fittings to the cylinder heads.

There had also been reports of rear passengers in Phantom Vs being uncomfortably warm because of the proximity of the large exhaust pipe under the bodywork. The pipe was re-routed through the chassis. 5 AT 34 had this treatment in autumn 1961. Later in the life of this chassis the rear springs were replaced after problems with the original set. But, generally speaking, the cars were a tremendous improvement on their predecessors and soon became great favourites.

It was extremely difficult to tell the two 'Canberras' apart, until one eagle-eyed chauffeur spotted that the earlier Phantom had a shorter skirt at the front under the number plate which concealed the power-steering ram; the later car had a full-length affair extending the width of the chassis behind the bumper.

With their good turn of speed, air-conditioning and power-steering, both of the new cars were obvious candidates for overseas tours and one of the first was for 5 AS 33 which in 1961 went out to Italy for a State Visit. It was in Turin that an accident happened where both front wings were scraped; and later the boot was dented.

In 1963 Her Majesty paid a visit to Australia and New Zealand. For the purpose the number one car (5 AT 34) was shipped out on board *Britannia*. It was the original intention as well to use the car in New Zealand, but it was learned that the Government there had spent a colossal amount on re-furbishing their ceremonial car fleet and so it was felt politic to keep 5 AT 34 on board. Pride of place in New Zealand therefore went to the two

ABOVE *Prince Charles obscured behind the result of a beer bottle thrown during a visit to the north east of England.*

RIGHT *In 1966 during a visit to Northern Ireland a piece of concrete was thrown at the Queen's car. This shows the result of a very rapid temporary repair made during the visit.*

new Phantom Vs they had just purchased. Australia had four years previously taken delivery of the two Hooper cabriolets and they also had four Silver Wraith limousines and two of the latest Silver Cloud III four-door cabriolets. (Interestingly both cars retained the SC II headlamp arrangements.) Despite being so well catered for, Her Majesty did have the opportunity to use her own car and also did so during a short visit to Fiji.

As on previous tours the 1963 visit was monitored throughout by Rolls-Royce, who obtained the services of Alan Lowe from their distributors York Motors in Australia. He was made a member of the Royal Tour car unit and worked hand in hand with John Rowe who a few years earlier had been on the Tour of Ghana. Along the route all the retailers were notified as well as the local offices of suppliers such as Lucas, Dunlop and Smiths.

Like its sister car, 5 AT 34 also suffered accident damage and had to be returned to the coachbuilders on its return to the United Kingdom. In an effort to reduce costs following some expensive repairs, the Crown Equerry

Both the Phantom IV and the Phantom V were flown out for the 1977 Jubilee Review visit to the British Army of the Rhine. Her Majesty is about to leave the parade ground in the Phantom V with the Phantom IV in the background.

wondered if it might be possible to have the Royal fleet maintained at a Ministry of Transport establishment, but because of the specialized nature of the coachwork and the mechanics the idea was not pursued.

It was in the middle of 1966 that the spectre of the Queen's safety was raised. On a visit to Belfast, Northern Ireland, a youth threw a piece of concrete weighing some nine pounds at the procession from a fifth or sixth floor. The missile actually struck the area just behind the mascot on the Royal car and then slid into the roadway. The Queen had seen the missile falling from the building and was pretty convinced, like most others, that if the block had hit the Perspex section of the roof it would have come through. Afterwards, Her Majesty remarked that Rolls-Royces were strong cars and added wryly that she was not too perturbed and that she understood it to be an expected but unusual hazard . . . Despite The Queen's insouciance over the affair, Rolls-Royce were keen to investigate the strengthening of the transparent section of the roof; in this, they were urged on by the Crown Equerry Lt Col. John Miller. An investigation was carried out by the Royal Aircraft Establishment who had previously dealt with bird-strikes to jet aircraft, Perspex canopies, and it may be assumed that an improvement was made to both of the Canberras at the time.

In 1974 an Austin Princess limousine in the Royal colours with Princess Anne and Captain Mark Philips on board was halted in The Mall by a deranged assailant. Following this incident all the Royal cars were fitted with an item long in use in many ordinary vehicles, a radio telephone. Later on, after the arrival of centralized locking on even more humble cars this too was incorporated. Although originally not fitted with rear view mirrors to the interior, it was eventually decided to fit a single stem with two mirrors to the centre of the dashboard capping rail which enabled both the detective and the chauffeur to keep an eye on following traffic.

Until 1978 both 'Canberras' were averaging about 6,000 miles a year but with the delivery of the new Phantom VI the annual mileage for both cars dropped. In the three decades since delivery, both cars have had regular maintenance which has involved re-painting and re-trimming of the interior. These were the vehicles that transformed Royal motor travel; they have now covered well over 120,000 miles each without major problems.

7

JUBILEE PRESENT FROM THE MOTOR INDUSTRY

'OIL BARREL'
Phantom VI Chassis number PGH 101

FROM 1952 WHEN THE AUSTIN PRINCESS with a Vanden Plas body was announced, there was always a pair in the Royal Mews. They were changed for the latest model when required – in 1958, 1964 and, finally, in 1968. This last date was the final production year for the model. There must have been considerable resistance to re-equipping with the recently announced Daimler DS 420, as virtually the last Princesses to be built were allocated to the Royal Mews. The cars were quite standard apart from electric windows and division, the provision for a blue light over the windscreen, and an aperture in the roof for holding a heraldic shield and standard.

As Jubilee year approached, demands on the Royal Mews were such that the Princesses were in common use either as secondary cars carrying the Royal Household or for minor public engagements. Despite quite frequent attention by Kennings, the London main agents for the marque, the pair of cars were showing the sort of malaise that hard-worked, less expensively engined cars can display. After nine years it looked as if there might be a need to expand the limousine fleet, especially as the two younger Princes, Andrew and Edward, would eventually require more formal transport.

Out of the blue came the generous suggestion by the Society of Motor Manufacturers and Traders (SMMT) to present The Queen in Jubilee

Not all the Royal cars were Rolls-Royce or Daimler. Early in The Queen's reign this Austin Princess (one of a pair) is leaving Buckingham Palace behind the first of the Phantom IVs of the Royal fleet.

year with a gift of a new Rolls-Royce, a Silver Shadow I I, for her personal use. This idea was communicated to Her Majesty who reportedly remarked that it seemed a great deal of money to spend on a car for her private enjoyment. At her suggestion, an approach was made to the S M M T to determine whether they would mind if the money was put towards a car that Her Majesty might use publicly, where it would have wider appreciation.

The Queen may not have realized that the only car she could use as an extension of her work would be almost twice as expensive as the Silver Shadow I I then on offer. . . The only vehicle that could possibly emerge as suitable for public occasions would be a Phantom. One can be pretty sure that Rolls-Royce would have been very reluctant at this stage to allow any other make to share their position as suppliers of the State Transport to Her Majesty. As Rolls-Royce were going to be involved if a Phantom was chosen they could, no doubt, absorb much of the below-the-line costs of the car's construction. And if they used the car to launch some new developments on the Phantom V I chassis, the press exposure would be beneficial. So the S M M T concurred with the Palace's suggestion and agreed to present the Queen during her Jubilee with a new working car – a Phantom V I.

At the time of the S M M T decision, the Phantom V I was being produced in small numbers using the G M Hydramatic gearbox which had

introduced Rolls-Royce to automatic driving in 1952. There had been an update to the 1959 chassis in 1968 when the car was given the early series Silver Shadow engine. Since the Phantom's introduction nearly 10 years before, the engine had been virtually unchanged, with the sparking plugs on the 'B' bank being rather inaccessible below the exhaust manifold. However, for the Phantom VI series the revised Silver Shadow engine, bringing the sparking plugs above the manifold, was used. Air conditioning became standard for both front and rear compartments.

The experimental department at Crewe were already testing a Phantom in which was installed the silver Shadow II engine and the GM 400 automatic transmission. Because there was no reasonable way of obtaining a drive from this three-speed gearbox to the old Hispano-Suiza type servo braking system, it was decided to use the Silver Shadow's high pressure hydraulic system to activate the brakes, but the old type drums were retained.

One result of the new set-up was that the time-lag betwcen application and activation was reduced; 'instant braking' could now be obtained! With the old type servo action the car needed to travel almost a foot before the brakes acted. Ordinarily this was of no consequence, but in very close manoeuvring it could be very disconcerting. With the new engine went

A Mulliner Park Ward artist's impression of the proposed new State limousine.

115

tamper-proof carburettors and a throw-away filter. All the engine refinements were to appear on the Silver Shadow II due to be introduced to the public in March of Jubilee year.

The work was done on the Queen's new Phantom VI, chassis PGH 101, paved the way for a number of improvements to the production Phantom from that chassis onwards. Only about a dozen a year were being hand-assembled, and at this time there were perhaps half a dozen Phantom VIs in European showrooms without owners . . . Fortunately, the position later became much healthier.

It is seemingly odd, bearing in mind all the improvements, which many considered amounted to more than those that changed the Phantom V into a Phantom VI, that the GM 400 model, as it became known at Mulliner Park Ward, did not get a Phantom VII designation. However, a new model type would have meant seeking type approval. This would have required the complete destruction of a car for the certification process. The company had turned down such a requirement for selling the car in the US and bearing in mind the very small quantities the car sold at, it was decided the car should remain Phantom VI. On the coachwork side there were also a number of modifications. Centralized locking, new fog-lights, new-type electric window lift cut-outs, and a revised facia which gave the driver a check column of warning lights.

Though it was planned to deliver the new Phantom VI to Her Majesty in 1977, her Jubilee year, sadly, industrial action hit not only Crewe but also Hythe Road where Mulliner Park Ward were assembling the car. Although the car was going through the works in secrecy, it must have been fairly obvious who the car was intended for, 'Rolls-Royce gave it a code-name

LEFT *Work in hand on the coachwork during the later stages of production at Hythe Road.*

OVERLEAF *The new State car ready to be handed over to the Queen. Note the rather out-of-character wing mirrors. They were very soon replaced by others of circular pattern.*

anyway'. The one chosen seems unusual, – it was called 'Oil Barrel', presumably to fox inquisitive folk into thinking it was for a Middle East potentate.

As this was the first Royal Rolls-Royce designed for the Queen since the emergence of the 'Canberras' in 1960, a great deal of effort was put into producing a first-class ceremonial vehicle. After all, it was most likely that it would still be conveying The Queen on her Golden Jubilee some twenty-five years hence. One can't help feeling that the company hoped that the new car might attract an order for a subsequent car.

Early in the design stage, a coloured drawing was submitted to the Palace which illustrated a Phantom VI with a more raked windscreen and a slightly lowered roofline. This would certainly have given the limousine a more dashing appearance, especially as the raking would have been carried through to all the roof pillars. But the request came back that the car should match up as closely as possible to the Phantom V design in the Royal Mews.

There were, however, two immediately noticeable structural differences. It would have been a retrograde step to have produced the new Phantom with the old-type single headlamp. Although the frontal aspect of the contemporary limousine was preserved, paired headlamps did not look as incongruous on the coachbuilt body as might have been thought at first. In a curious reversion to the old Mk I Phantom V elevation, the old type boot compartment lid was retained. This was in fact a necessity, as the more razor-edged treatment of the current model did not lend itself to the fitment of the Perspex dome cover into the boot.

Sadly, because of safety regulations, the rear-hinged rear doors were replaced with forward-hinged doors. This presents certain problems for photographers for the simple reason that as the Royal Car approaches, all lenses focus on the rear compartment and this is then obscured by the person deputed to open the door. So with the new Phantom VI the car has to draw a little further on so that when Her Majesty alights she is unobscured. With the old rear-hinged doors this presented no problem as the centre of the car could be lined up with the place chosen as the halt, and of course the detective could slip out of the forward-hinged front door as the car stopped, ready to open the rear door.

There is really no satisfactory way of improving on the old rear-hangers, which Sir Henry Royce advocated as being the best system of protecting passengers as they alighted from his cars. Certainly, the present system can produce a shambles, as happened when the new car was used on the occasion of the 40th anniversary of the D-Day landings in 1984. Her Majesty was driven a little further on to allow the photographers to get good shots of The Queen alighting, but the gentlemen of the Press took this as a sign that the car was not going to stop and scampered after the vehicle. From now on, instead of that noble prow framing picture, the rear aspect of the car as often as not is in view.

The interior of PGH 101 was also the subject of some changes and these were certainly an improvement. Between the chauffeur and detective was placed a telephone handset; this was normally out of sight where the centre armrest might have been. The phone's coiled cable was long enough

Press interest in the new car was tremendous, as may be judged from this photograph of photographers at work!

LEFT *Once more, the rear armrest houses several important features, including a push-button radio and a separate tape player. The buttons at the top are air conditioning controls.*

BELOW LEFT *Lift the lid on the armrest and it discloses a pivoting vanity mirror and pocket dictaphone, complete with spare batteries.*

ABOVE RIGHT *It is usual that the driver's handbook for any particular model is applicable to very many cars. Not so in this case. This car had a handbook unique to itself. As this reproduction of the title page shows, it is only for the Rolls-Royce Phantom PGH 101; an example of an inside page (RIGHT) shows details of the armrest, which is unlike that fitted to any other car.*

By Appointment to
Her Majesty The Queen
Motor Car Manufacturers
Rolls-Royce Motors Limited

Rolls-Royce Phantom

Car serial number PGH 101

CONTROLS AND INSTRUMENTS

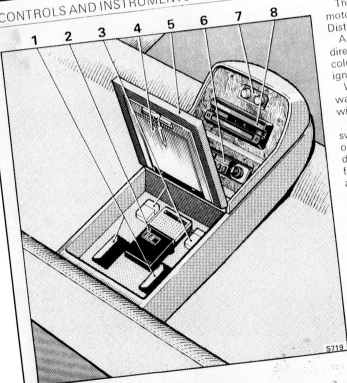

Fig.14   Rear Seat Centre Arm Rest
1 Spare cassettes for dictation machine
2 Dictation machine
3 Spare batteries for dictation machine
4 Mirror
5 Compartment lid
6 Radio
7 Change-over switches for air conditioning unit
8 Stereo cassette tape deck

The wipers are self parking when switched off. If the wiper motor continues to operate after being switched off consult a Distributor or Retailer.

A second switch marked WASH is mounted in the end of the direction indicator lever on the left-hand side of the steering column (see Fig.13). This switch will operate only when the ignition switch is in either the accessories or 'ignition on' position.

When the windscreen wipers are in motion and the push button washer switch is depressed, fluid will be directed onto the windscreen until the switch is released.

When the windscreen wipers are stationary and the washer switch is depressed the windscreen wipers and washer will operate, and will continue to operate as long as the switch is depressed. On release of the switch the washer will cease to function while the windscreen wipers will continue for approximately four strokes to complete the cleaning operation.

If the intermittent wiping system is in operation and the washer switch is depressed the windscreen wipers and washer will operate. On release of the push button switch the system will automatically revert back to the intermittent operation.

Fluid from the windscreen washer jets should be directed onto the windscreen towards the top of the arc traversed by the wiper blades. If fluid is not delivered through the jets check that there is fluid in the reservoir and that the jets are not obstructed (see page 95).

Instrument lamps and panel illumination switch

The instrument lamps and panel illumination are controlled by a switch on the facia marked PANEL LIGHT (see Fig.13) ; the lamps will operate only when the main lighting switch is on.

The switch control has two clockwise positions from the off position. The first clockwise position of the switch control provides dim illumination of the instruments ; the second clockwise position provides bright illumination.

Air conditioning controls

The air conditioning system in the front compartment and the air conditioning system in the rear compartment operate independently of each other. It is necessary for the ignition to be switched on for operation of either system.

---

*The Queen and the Duke of Edinburgh at the official opening of
the huge Arrow Park Hospital. They travelled in the
Phantom VI.*

---

for it to be passed over the lowered division for the use of the rear
compartment occupants. Because of the nature of the radio telephone it was
not possible to have the antenna on an electrically operated retractable rod;
instead, the aerial can either be fixed or unfixed in a matter of seconds from
its position on the 'saddle' of the boot (just behind the rear window) and
stored in the luggage compartment.

There had been technical advances since refrigeration was first fitted to
the 'Canberras' more than 16 years earlier, and for a more efficient air
conditioning system, a grill was installed on the top of the saddle just behind
where the Perspex dome ended. To power all the ancillaries a 95 amp/hr

battery was fitted and, for the first time on a Royal car, an alternator. Also new as original equipment was a stereo-cassette player coupled to a MW and LW radio; and a miniature tape recorder with its own batteries was fitted behind the in-car entertainment set within a lidded compartment to the centre armrest. The armrest also contained a rather large mirror which could be hinged either left or right when placed in the upright position. As on the previous Phantom Vs, the headroom was $51\frac{1}{2}$ in. from floor to ceiling in the rear compartment.

Upholstery in the front compartment was the same as on the other Royal cars – that is to say navy blue. The seats were in navy blue leather but normally they were covered with cloth of the same colour which could be removed for cleaning. The carpets at the front were also blue and had black rubber inserts in the heel areas. However it was in the rear compartment that the biggest change came, for instead of the usual rather dull grey cloth, a new scheme called Baroda Blue was used and this was matched by a piercing blue (called Mountain Blue) lambswool rug; underneath, the carpet matched the colour exactly.

Quite a lot of the Park Ward men who had worked on the first 'Canberras' were still with the company after their amalgamation with H. J. Mulliner and amongst them, working on the latest vehicle, was Roy Aldridge, then superintendant of the Special Bodies Section. His handiwork can be seen in the special metal fittings for air vents, boot-lid handle and lock and the standard-holder, which, after being fashioned in brass were heavily chrome-plated.

The paint scheme for the new Phantom VI – soon to become Her Majesty's No. 1 State car – was, as previously, black over Royal Claret.

Although it had been hoped to finish the car in Jubilee year, the industrial action and the further development work on the car delayed delivery until Spring 1978. The new State car was handed over in the presence of Her Majesty as her Jubilee Gift at a small ceremony at Windsor Castle.

Her Majesty must have an eye for symmetry because within a few moments she had noticed that whereas the other State cars had circular rear-view wing mirrors the latest car was fitted with the production rectangular variety. The old ones were no longer being manufactured. The new ones were untinted; the older ones had a slight green tint which cut down glare from following traffic. A search throughout the country was started for a pair and, surprisingly, two surfaced in a drawer at Hythe Road where the new car had started its life . . .

'Oil Barrel' is at the present time the fastest high-roofed Royal car for State duties in the Royal Mews and also the most economical with the ECE consumption figures of 10 mpg around town, 15 mpg at a constant 56 mph and just under 13 mpg at 70 mph. At its initial 3,000 miles service, a matter of months after delivery, the opportunity was taken to instal a grab-handle to the nearside door capping rail. Apparently the detective had experienced difficulty closing the door with the armrest-cum-handgrip which was rather low down.

The first big overseas tour for the Phantom VI was in the middle of 1978 when Her Majesty paid a State Visit to the Federal Republic of Germany. As on previous occasions, it was decided that when not accompanied by her German hosts she would use her own car. The Tour, held over the better part of a week, was unfortunately subjected to rather vicious weather. But the car made quite an impression on the West German Press and Rolls-Royce sales to the country increased for some time afterwards. Chassis PGH 101 had been driven over to West Germany via the Channel ferry and routed through Belgium into the Federal Republic. On the trip was John Rowe, who shortly afterwards was promoted to the position of service manager at Hythe Road, where he remained until 1983 when he went to Conduit Street. He later joined the R-R distributors Arnett of Bournemouth.

In 1980 Her Majesty went to Italy. The car was motored across Europe to await her arrival. One of her most important engagements was a visit to the Vatican City. To collect The Queen from the airport the car was driven at speed down the *autostrada*. The ever-solicitious Italian police laid on a police escort for the car which was driven by the Queen's senior chauffeur, the colourful Harold Purvey. The Alfa Romeos, one in front and one behind, were travelling with the Royal car at speeds hovering around 100 mph when there was an extraordinary mishap. The transparent dome at the back of the Royal car broke away and sailed into the air, to come crashing down on the road and shatter. The following police car narrowly avoided the wreckage and the convoy came to a skidding halt. One of the police cars collected the remains and Mr Purvey, somewhat shaken by the event, pressed on accompanied by the nonplussed Rolls-Royce representative. For her visit to the Pope the Queen travelled in her car with the black dome-cover in position.

Naturally Rolls-Royce and their coachbuilders were eager to find out what had happened; after all, in 20 years, no other car had been affected in this way. After some extensive enquiries and overcoming some understandable reluctance to be in any way connected with the ill-fortune of the event, they soon found the explanation.

It is more than likely that when the accident happened at around 100 mph the chauffeur or his companion had opened his window for one reason or another. It is thought the division was retracted and the in-rush of air pressure at speed in the heat had simply blown the Perspex dome cover out of its seal. Up to this time the dome had been fixed to the body by tight rubber channels and liberal applications of bonding sealant. Following this incident it was decided, naturally, to improve on the system of attachment. Nowadays the dome is sealed to the rubber channels with a polysulphide solution and the rubber channels sealed to the bodywork with the same substance. The Royal chauffeurs are also advised not to drive too fast without putting the metal top in place as it would seem that, without it, a vacuum could be created over the roof which might lead to it lifting off.

Now with the total mileage around the 40,000 mile mark, the Phantom VI is averaging around 6,000 miles a year and there can't be that many places in the United Kingdom to which it has not travelled. It is normal for a Phantom V 'Canberra' to accompany it and indeed the No.2 car is 5 AT 34. It is with this pair of cars that Her Majesty normally undertakes most of her engagements. The other three cars, chassis 5 AS 33, PMH 10415 and 4 AF 2, are kept either for duties with the younger Royal Family or are marshalled as the following car. With these five Rolls-Royces, the Royal Family undertake their principal engagements throughout the year with reliability and distinction.

8

THE LAST ROYAL PHANTOM?

'LADY NORFOLK'
Phantom VI Chassis number PMH 10415

ROLLS-ROYCE HAD BEEN CAMPAIGNING to renew the State cars at the Palace since they offered to take back the Phantom IVs after the delivery of the second 'Canberra' in 1961, but it was to be another 25 years before the Palace purchased a new Rolls-Royce. The Silver Jubilee gift from the SMMT delivered in 1978 had come at a very opportune moment, with many of the younger members of the Royal Family now making claims on the official car fleet.

By 1985 the Phantom VI build line, if it could be called such, was producing about three to four cars a year. The cost of a new Phantom was a dizzy £200,000, and a specialized body would increase that even more. A State Landaulette delivered to the King of Malaya in 1986 was reputed to have cost close to £315,000 and that was without UK tax. Although efforts had been made to keep the Civil List (payment to The Queen for her position as Head of State) in line with inflation, this has plainly not happened. As a simple yardstick, the cost of a new State Car in 1952 when Her Majesty came to the throne was approximately £4,600 and this amounted to under 1% of Her Majesty's then Civil List of £475,000. In the late 1980s, with the cost of a specialized State car running at about £300,000 this amounted to around 6% of the Civil List, which had risen to just over £5,250,000.

Despite the efforts by the Royal Mews to maintain the Royal fleet of cars as economically as possible it became obvious that there would have to

The 1954 Phantom IV, 'Jubilee', just after completion.
Five years were to pass before it was purchased by the Queen.
Of course, the number plates were then discarded.

FAR LEFT *A look at the chauffeur's compartment of the Phantom VI delivered in Spring, 1978; notice the twin interior mirrors, one for the driver and one for the detective. Seat belts, radio telephone and fire extinguisher were all parts of the original specification.*

ABOVE AND LEFT *For the 'Jubilee' Phantom VI, the colour of the cloth upholstery was changed from grey to Baroda blue, with the carpet in Mountain blue. The pull-out step protruding from the seat helps access for adjustment to the roof fitments.*

BELOW *A recent photograph of the Queen Mother's Phantom V, delivered in 1962, showing its current splendid condition. It displays the 'Britannia' mascot and, for once, is seen with the head folded down.*

RIGHT *Her Majesty Queen Elizabeth the Queen Mother's mascot, Britannia atop the globe. It was originally made for King George V's Royal Daimlers.*

OVERLEAF *Carrying the heraldic shield of the Duke of Edinburgh, the Prince who ordered the car more than 40 years earlier, Phantom IV (Chassis 4 AF 2) gleams immaculate as ever in the Royal Mews.*

BELOW *The Elegant roof fitments on Princess Margaret's 1967 Silver Shadow*

LEFT *Princess Margaret's Silver Shadow, from an experimental run of 20 long-wheelbase cars built in 1967.*

BELOW LEFT *Princess Margaret's 1975 Silver Shadow (Chassis LRH 21379) photographed after it had passed into private hands, having been replaced by a Silver Wraith II.*

RIGHT *Hooper advertising, the Royal warrant prominent. It is impossible to know whether the words 'By Appointment to H M the King' actually made any difference to potential customers. What is probably more apparent is the adverse effect of losing a pre-eminent and very visible Royal association; consider the Daimler company history.*

BELOW *The prominent brightwork on the Duke of Gloucester's 1951 Phantom IV makes it particularly attractive. (The present owner, Lesley Smith, has a substantial collection of Rolls-Royce cars at his home near Bury).*

A matter of choice . . .

"He that makes the shoe can't tan the leather," and so for leather, as for all the materials used in Hooper coachwork, we ask the finest craftsmen to give of their best. They offer a selection, we make our choice, and the owner indicates his preference. Only individually selected cowhides, tanned, dressed

and dyed in fast colours by age-old methods are ever considered. A sample is reproduced as the background of this page.

Thus, the owner's wishes are faithfully interpreted in every refinement of a Hooper body, while its construction, craftsmanship and finish remain unquestionably Hooper. The beauty of its flowing lines, the feel of its first-quality materials, even that unmistakable sound as its doors are closed are all Hooper hallmarks, but the grain of a veneer, the colour of upholstery, the very dimensions and angle of seats — these are decided by the customer. He determines the shade of a paint, Hooper skill dictates the quality of finish.

The wide, curved windscreen provides a
remarkably unrestricted angle of vision

HOOPER *Uncommonly fine coachwork*

Hooper Saloon on Bentley Mk. VI
Design No. 8282

HOOPER AND COMPANY
(COACHBUILDERS) LIMITED
Established 1807

LEFT *H M The Queen, accompanied by a lady-in-waiting, travel in the premier State car, the 1978 Phantom VI, a Jubilee gift from the Society of Motor Manufacturers and Traders.*

BELOW *The late King Olaf of Norway on a State visit, accompanied by Prince Philip, arriving at the Home Park in the number 2 State car.*

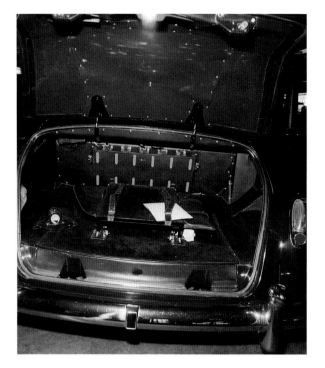

ABOVE AND LEFT *Some details of the 'Canberra' cars ; the photographs were taken at the same time as 'Jubilee' was being built, in 1976.*

RIGHT *Royal Phantoms IV, V and VI ; coachwork by H J Mulliner, Park Ward and Mulliner Park Ward respectively. A pretty syllogism, and fascinating image of seamless evolution.*

H R H Prince Michael of Kent's Phantom VI, acquired in 1981. Finished in Oxford blue with a gold coachline, the car's badge bar was pretty well compulsory for the President of the RAC!

be an update at some time. There was the thought too that imminent legislation would make the wearing of seat belts by rear seat passengers compulsory before the end of the decade. By the middle of 1985 it had been decided to purchase a Phantom VI and retire the Phantom IV State landaulette. Pressure on the Royal Mews meant that it would be difficult to maintain a State fleet for members of the Royal Family other than the Queen if there were less than five State cars available. Although Prince Charles had use of a long wheelbase Bentley Turbo this was not really suitable on more sombre occasions. If he purchased a Phantom VI then of course he would be liable for purchase tax on such a car.

Negotiations between financial advisers to the Palace and the liaison official at Rolls-Royce, Roger Cra'ster, eventually produced a contract for a standard-roofed Phantom VI, but with special modifications. Peter Wharton, who had joined Park Ward in 1934 and retired in 1979, was persuaded with little difficulty, to involve himself with his fourth car for the British Monarch. In the autumn of 1985 he prepared a wash-drawing of the car showing exterior treatment and also one of the area over the rear compartment to illustrate a glass-roof insert. These were presented to the Palace and were accepted, apart from the paint treatment to the boot-lid.

To keep costs down, a standard roof was ordered, but two alterations helped visibility. First, the rear quarter-lights were extended rearwards about six inches, which necessitated re-routing the air-conditioning pipes to the roof outlets further back into the quarters. Secondly, a glass section was let into the roof over the main rear seats. The rear end of the interior trimming now extended right above the main seats and reduced even further the already critical head room of $37\frac{1}{2}$ ins, to about 36 ins. This was such a reduction, especially for taller members of the Royal Family, that in March 1988 the car was returned to Mulliner Park Ward for the rear seat to be lowered 2 ins to compensate. For privacy, an electrically operated shutter could obscure the glass panel in the roof and two covers could clip over the extended rear quarter lights. A further innovation was another cover complete with a postbox-size aperture in the centre, which could be clipped over the rear back-light. All three covers were normally kept in the car's boot when not in use.

ABOVE *The final drawing by Peter Wharton of the interior of the new Phantom V I. In particular it shows the extended quarter lights that would improve visibility, and the perspex roof panel with its sliding blind.*

BELOW *Peter Wharton's illustration of the exterior, as submitted to Buckingham Palace. This could well be the very last ever Rolls-Royce Phantom produced for the Monarch.*

Again to reduce costs, the rear boot-lid handle was a standard casting and not the normal Royal vertical handle; (a pity this because it does not match the other Phantoms in the fleet). Again both front and rear bumpers were made detachable to enable the 19 ft 10 in. length to be reduced by some 12 in. so as to fit *Britannia*'s garage. Like the other Phantoms, the car was fitted with a police light above the windscreen, a shield aperture behind it and at the back of that a small trapdoor to erect the Royal Standard. For communication with the outside world there were a pair of electric aerials either side of the front wing for front and rear radios, and a de-mountable whip aerial for the radio-telephone which was positioned in the rear saddle behind the backlight.

The car's interior followed the colour scheme for the previous Phantom V I; that is to say Baroda Blue cloth for the rear compartment and navy blue for the front. Another mountain blue rug in lambswool allowed rear seat occupants to enjoy the comfort of its deep pile. The centre armrest contains a large mirror which folds out of view inside the rest itself; also covered from prying eyes; the changeover switch for the air-conditioning which can be operated from either of the side armrests. Under a veneered cover on the left

side are controls for the radio, and above are switches to operate the division, glass roof shutter, normal internal lights and also the strip lighting for more formal occasions. In connection with the latter, there is now more space in the boot by virtue of the miniaturization of the strip-light invertors which, now take up only a quarter of the space of those previously fitted.

The chauffeur's compartment is fitted with a Radiomobile set, a radio-telephone to keep contact with the outside world, master control of the windows, central locking and other security items. As before, the detective occupying the left front seat can raise the Royal Standard by pushing it up through a trap-door in the roof. The chauffeur has the benefit of a step to help mount (or dismount) the heraldic shield from the roof.

As document space is at a premium in such a vehicle, the rear compartment doors were for the first time fitted with slip-pockets. For the first and only time since the delivery of the now retired landaulette, the face-forward occasional seats were made to meet in the middle when erected, as there is no cabinet on this car to obstruct the wider seats. The rear seat occupants have a clear view of a slim-line clock let into the back of the division waist-rail.

The latest Phantom VI was test driven for some 1,600 miles prior to delivery on July 23, 1987. The greatest problem facing the planners had been how to accommodate the distribution of the Royal Claret and Black. Previous cars had had a natural break line at the base of the rear quarter lights where the perspex top and cover was fitted, on this car the black had to be given a swaged line to meet the Royal Claret just over the boot saddle, not the most satisfactory solution but the only one available.

After the completion of the road testing, the car had the rear doors and boot-lid painted with Her Majesty's Crest surrounded by the Garter of Britain's principal order of knighthood. Geoffrey Frances – who had painted the first one on Her Majesty's Phantom IV when she was The Princess Elizabeth, Duchess of Edinburgh – emerged from his south coast retirement home to paint them. A special kneeling Spirit of Ecstasy mascot which could be detached with ease (so that it could be replaced with St George and the dragon) was also made up.

It is rather difficult to imagine where in the car hierarchy the new car fits. The Princess of Wales has used this Phantom and must have noticed the difference in interior height when getting into and out of the car; the older cars are certainly more elegant to emerge from on public engagements. The 1978 high roof-line car remains the number one State car and the 1961 Phantom V follows it; the new car probably fits in the pecking order at number five. One couldn't imagine it being followed by a high roof-line Phantom V or VI on any public engagement.

It is possible bearing this in mind, that when the 1950 Phantom IV (the oldest car in the Royal Mews) is retired, another high roof-line Phantom VI may be commissioned: almost certainly for the last time, as the Phantom build-line is to close in 1992, although it is thought that a chassis could be obtained for HM, if requested, for some years yet.

The 'Lady Norfolk', looking resplendent as delivered to the Royal Mews.

9

THE QUEEN MOTHER BECOMES
A ROLLS-ROYCE OWNER

'STIRLING'
Phantom V Chassis number 5 CG 37

FOR MUCH OF HER PUBLIC LIFE Her Majesty Queen Elizabeth The Queen Mother remained a devotee of the Daimler marque. Prior to the King's death in February 1952, no cars were registered in her name but after that Her Majesty acquired a number of vehicles. On her husband's death the Queen Mother took over one of the 1949 Daimler Straight Eights and this was augmented by another Straight Eight, which had been a Daimler Royal stock vehicle, in August 1954. Less than a year later The Queen Mother purchased a Hooper-bodied Daimler DK 400 for private engagements. This last car was registered NLT 1, her 1949 car was given NLT 2 and the 1949 ex-Royal stock Daimler, NLT 6. Since the mid-1950s there has been quite a lot of shuffling around in The Queen Mother's Mews but those number plates have remained allocated to her. Around this time Her Majesty also purchased a Jaguar Mk VII and this was progressively uprated by Jaguar to Mk VIII and Mk IX configuration.

Despite her faith in Daimler, the Queen Mother did purchase a Rolls-Royce when the time came to retire her 1949 State car. Her Majesty disposed of her Daimler NLT 6 in late 1959 and for a short time took over one of the Royal Mews Daimlers which was registered in the name of her Comptroller. So from 1959 until 1961 The Queen Mother had back in her possession two of the cars ordered by her late husband. She was, however, about to follow her daughter's example and have a Rolls-Royce as her principal car.

The order for the Rolls-Royce Phantom V was made in the late summer of 1961 and the chassis was received by the coachbuilder Park Ward on November 17, with delivery promised for the first week of February the following year. In December 1960 Park Ward had delivered a Phantom V landaulette to the Governor of Hong Kong and going through the works at the same time as the Queen Mother's car was a similarly-bodied vehicle for the President of Tunisia. As a matter of interest, all three of these cars remain in the hands of their original owners over 30 years later.

The State cars that Her Majesty had always favoured were landaulettes; and in the choice of body for her first and so far only Rolls-Royce, the Queen Mother requested this same style of coachwork. The Park Ward Design No.1104 differed from the Hong Kong and Tunisia cars in a number of minor respects, but the most obvious was in the glass section let into the roof just behind the division and in the rear compartment appointments. Like the other two landaulettes, the car was similar to the standard limousine body and only differed in the treatment to the rear; a landaulette head replacing the normal quarter panelling. The boot lid was given similar treatment to her daughter's Phantoms, that is to say the handle was placed vertically, instead of horizontally as on production Park Ward limousines.

This car had to be registered, so a number plate was built into the boot-lid and provision was made between the front over-riders to fit a matching plate. Externally, the car was finished in black over Royal Claret and in case the car should travel on *Britannia*, arrangements were made as on the 'Canberras' to reduce the valence between body and bumpers and the latter were made detachable.

Curiously, there were two omissions to the technical side of the coachwork in comparison with the earlier cars. One was that there was no provision for air-conditioning and the other was that the head leather to the rear was raised and lowered manually. The glass panel was, as previously, fitted with a blind which could be slid into place electrically, although there was a manual winder in case of failure in the motor-drive. Between the fixed

LEFT *The Queen Mother retained one of the State Daimlers from the Royal Mews in 1952, and she also acquired this one some two years later. It had been kept in stock by the Daimler Company for just such an eventuality. This car is now on display in a Berlin museum.*

BELOW *This early Phantom V landaulette was made for the President of Tunisia. The Queen used the car during a visit to that country in 1980.*

ABOVE *The Queen Mother's Rolls-Royce was completed in the early winter of 1962. This view of the rear clearly shows the high position of the rear number plate – a feature that has been said to spoil the lines of the car.*

RIGHT *Surprisingly, the folding head (or hood) could only be lowered manually, and looked a little untidy in the down position. The Hooper-built landaulette hoods folded lower and appeared neater.*

portion of the head and the front of the landaulette leather roof section, just in behind the Triplex glass panel, were fitted three fluorescent lights. These, coupled with two ordinary lights let into the flexible portion of the roof, provided adequate illumination at night. In the steps of the rear doors were fitted two concealed running board lights. In the recess under the wood-trim on either side of the rear compartment was a flexible reading light and below was fitted a leather notebook with silver propelling pencil and, just beyond, a leather-backed mirror with a cigarette lighter. Controls for the lights and heating were fitted into the offside recess, with the light switches duplicated in the nearside.

Internally the car was finished in mid-grey to the rear and navy blue in the front compartment, which was the colour scheme of the Royal Daimlers Her Majesty had used. The cross-banded walnut veneer was extended to a central cabinet behind the division which housed a recess for documents and space for a small tea service. The rear centre armrest housed the radio set which was normally concealed from view behind a lid, covered in the same material as the armrest. Unlike the radios supplied to the 'Canberras', the Queen Mother chose Plessey to install the radio set. The driver had the normal Radiomobile. Both sets were fitted with powered aerials.

At first it had been thought that a similar system as fitted to the Queen's cars would be used for erecting the Royal Standard. However in the end it was decided to mount the standard with the heraldic shield and not separately. The small blue light was fitted above the windscreen and the driver could flash the headlamps as necessary (it was not until late in 1961 that this facility was offered on other cars from Rolls-Royce). For engagements of a more private nature two panels could be taken from the boot and clipped over the rear quarter lights; these were black to the outside and grey to the interior. Finally, her Majesty's monogram encircled by the collar of the Order of the Garter, was applied to the rear doors and boot-lid, and her own mascot, Britannia atop the globe, was then fitted to a spare radiator cap.

Whereas for the Queen's first Phantom V it took eight months from chassis delivery to the completion of the car, in the Queen Mother's case it was less than three months; Christmas occurred half way through the car's construction. On February 9, 1962 the guarantee card was issued and the executive filling in the details at Conduit Street must have been slightly overcome by the occasion because he entered the first owner as 'Her Gracious Majesty Queen Elizabeth The Queen Mother'. Despite her position as the last Queen Consort to the final Emperor of India, I doubt if Her Majesty would lay claim to 'Gracious' as her official term of address, although of course anyone who has come into contact with Her immediately brings this adjective to mind.

Chassis 5 CG 37 which had progressed through Park Ward under the codename of 'Stirling' was issued with the old Royal stock Daimler number plate of N L T 6.

Later, when Her Majesty disposed of her Hooper-bodied Daimler D K 400 after nearly 20 years' service, the number of that car was transferred to 'Stirling' and so it became N L T 1. The Queen Mother had acquired a Daimler D S 420 limousine in 1970 and this was replaced in 1978 by a more up-to-date Daimler limousine which incorporated a unique fitment. Whereas on the Rolls-Royce the rear compartment floor is flat, that on the Daimler has a lip over which one has to climb. To assist rear passengers Her Majesty had a step fitted which automatically slides out from under the door-sill when the door is opened. All the Daimlers supplied after the arrival of the Rolls-Royce undertook private engagements and minor appointments while Phantom 5 CG 37 was kept for the major public undertakings.

Three years after delivery, 'Stirling' had its front springs changed and on its 10th birthday the engine was exchanged for a new unit. In the 1970s the car was fitted with side repeater lights on the wing and an extra pair of fog lamps were added beside those already on the fender. There has also been the expensive replacement of the head-leather to the rear compartment. Despite a mileage in excess of the Phantom Vs in the Royal Mews (well past 150,000) the car shows no outward sign of needing replacement and Her Majesty seems as pleased as ever with it. The cabinetwork, chrome, upholstery, carpets and bodywork are a tribute to those on her staff who work with the car. Maintenance has been carried out at Hythe Road, but with the Rolls-Royce service station's move to new premises the car has gone there too.

LEFT *There are plenty of interior lights to give good illumination for evening engagements. The two lever-catches keep the head in position and water-tight.*

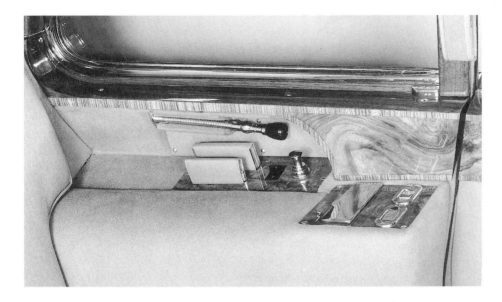

OVERLEAF *NLT 6 on a visit to Shrivenham in 1964; Her Majesty's Standard and Coat of Arms can be seen particularly well.*

ABOVE *The nearside armrest houses a flexible reading light, compact, writing paper and pencil, plus division control switch, light controls, cigarette lighter and ashtray. All these were duplicated on the other side.*

RIGHT *The steering column was given a very steep rake in order to maximize the available passenger space. This photograph was taken when construction was well advanced; the chalk marks on the pillar indicate areas needing further detailed attention.*

LEFT *With the glass roof panel uncovered, the interior appears bright and comfortable. Note the deep-pile lambswool rug and warm air grilles below the seat. Very unusual are the small tabs protruding slightly from both doors. When either one is pulled down it provides a convenient hook on which to hang a Royal hat.*

5 CG 37 has made a number of trips abroad, several to units of the British Army of the Rhine in West Germany. It was during such a visit in 1965 to the Black Watch at Minden, that a young NCO, Arthur Barty, took a photograph of the Queen Mother in her car, a shot that he still keeps. In 1978, then in the service of Her Majesty, Arthur Barty, as the deputy head chauffeur, drove the car to Germany for a visit by the Queen Mother to the unit to which he once belonged.

The head chauffeur is John Collins, who was appointed to that position at the early age of 28. There are three chauffeurs who have the responsibility of keeping the Queen Mother's State and private vehicles ready for duty at any time. Her Majesty has always had a number of 'characters' on her driving staff. One was Harold Fishburne who, though employed only on a temporary basis, was still sound enough in his judgement in his 70s to be in charge of the limousines. A particularly well-liked head chauffeur was Don Redwood, who worked for Her Majesty for a great many years.

The limousines have a busy life, often covering up to 500 miles from northern Scotland to London in as short a time as possible. It is also just as demanding for the chauffeurs, guiding the big cars down from the Queen Mother's Balmoral home, Birkhall, to her London residence at Clarence House. But all of her chauffeurs have a distinctive loyalty to The Queen Mother and give the impression that although their work can be arduous at times, very few would contemplate working across the way at the Palace.

Her Majesty the Queen Mother shows just as much reliability in her role as the State car she owns. One can only wish that, like her Rolls-Royce, Her Majesty will go on forever . . .

LEFT *In West Germany, during Her Majesty's visit to British troops, the car is guarded by two very smart looking soldiers of the Queen's Own Hussars. Notice that the headlamp lenses have been modified (by black patches) to make them suitable for continental driving.*

BELOW *The Queen Mother, sitting well forward in Her seat and with the window lowered so as to give spectators a better view. As the flags above the crowd indicate, this was during a visit to the RAF.*

LEFT *In the Mews at Marlborough House the landaulette is examined prior to overhaul in 1974.*

10

HRH THE PRINCESS MARGARET: A VERY GOOD CUSTOMER

'BARON MONTAIGNE'
Phantom IV Chassis number 4 BP 7
(and other Rolls-Royce cars)

PRINCESS MARGARET'S FIRST OFFICIAL STATE CAR was a Rolls-Royce Phantom IV, and to date she has been the Royal Family's most prolific owner of Rolls-Royce vehicles. The Princess now has her seventh car of that make, five of which have been from the Silver Shadow series.

Princess Margaret ordered her first car in autumn 1953 whilst she was still in residence at Clarence House with the Queen Mother. There are a number of references to her using Daimlers then in the possession of her Mother. In fact, Hoopers provided some special fitments for her use, including a loose cushion which Mr Clouting, one of the chauffeurs at Clarence House, took to the coachbuiders for re-trimming in grey cloth when the Royal stock Daimler's rear compartment was changed from dark blue cloth to grey. However, as the Princess undertook more engagements she decided that she should purchase a car of her own, and chose a Rolls-Royce Phantom IV, chassis 4 BP 7. It was given the code-name 'The Baron Montaigne'.

On January 4, 1954 the specification was issued and a mere five weeks later the chassis was delivered to H. J. Mulliner for the fitment of a seven passenger body. Princess Margaret, being very petite, could have experienced some difficulty if she had wished to drive herself because of its sheer size and weight. The chassis was the largest private vehicle then being built in Britain and did not have power steering. So, from the start, the coachbuilders made some discreet modifications and additions to help the Princess drive her own car, should she wish.

An automatic gearbox was installed; this gave finger-tip selection of the gears and did away with a gear lever and clutch. The steering position was made one inch shorter than standard and the column rake was set as high as possible. Mulliner's raised the driving seat cushion and backrest to accommodate the height of the owner and, in case they were ever needed, detachable extensions were made up to fit the brake and accelerator pedals.

The car's interior was trimmed throughout in fawn West of England cloth and the cabinetwork was in cross-banded walnut veneer. The windows, division, rear window blind and cover to the glass section over the rear compartment could all be operated electrically. For extra privacy the rear compartment quarter lights could be obscured with shutters which were normally concealed in the rear bodywork. The main seat could be raised or lowered a few inches with a small winder and the car was fitted with two face-forward occasional seats. In between them was a cabinet which housed a loudspeaker grille and heater outlet and below that a lidded storage compartment; although at a later stage this was removed to allow the extra passengers to swivel around without jamming their feet against the lower part of the cabinet. Above the cabinet was a pair of cigarette lighters and let into the division rail was a clock.

Unusually, a matching set of picnic tables let down from above each occasional seat. For the use of the main seat occupants there was a lidded compartment with a mirror set into the centre arm-rest. The offside armrest contained a Radiomobile set similar to that fitted in the Phantom IV landaulette then going through Hoopers, and this could be concealed with a chromium plated shutter. Both offside and nearside armrest wood trims contained a cigarette lighter and an ashtray, and just below them, a reading light was fitted.

Considerable thought was given to the heating arrangements on the car, with a heater below the rear seat, switched on and operated from either the front or rear compartments. Heat was also shared between the compartments by a heater situated under the front passenger seat. Finally, fresh air could be admitted through aircraft-type inlets either side of the back of the division. The normal demisting arrangements applied of course to the front windscreen and the electrical demisting of the small rear window.

As mentioned, there was a separate radio set in the rear, but it shared an under-floor aerial with the front compartment radio. When the rear set was in use the front set became inoperative. For official and public engagements the blue light above the centre of the windscreen could be switched on and just behind it was a clamp which held a rearward facing light which shone on to the Princess's heraldic shield. The result was a veritable cat's cradle, so early on in the car's career it was changed to the Lucas integral system.

Princess Margaret's car introduced something new to Royal motoring and that concerned flying her personal standard. Instead of the chauffeur having to get out of the car, all he had to do was to open a trap-door in the roof which enabled the standard to be pushed through and rotated into place. Because of this a special chain drive to the Triplex glass section cover had to be used; this did not intrude too far over the heads of the front compartment occupants.

Whilst the car was being constructed Rolls-Royce fitted a new type of production pinion to the rear axle. All was now ready for 'The Baron Montaigne' to take his bow. Complete with the new type of over-rider soon to be fitted to the Silver Cloud series, 4 B P 7 was driven off to Clarence House.

The eight-cylinder Phantom I V was delivered to the Princess on July 16, 1954, about a fortnight later than promised, but Rolls-Royce had incorporated a great many new ideas into the car which eventually found their way into other ceremonial vehicles. The car joined the Queen Mother's Daimlers in the mews at the rear of Queen Mary's old home, Marlborough House.

'The Baron Montaigne' remained Princess Margaret's official car for some 12 years and was the car that was most often trailed by eager

ABOVE *Modifications to standard specification so that Princess Margaret could, if she wished, drive the car herself, included a more upright and shorter steering column, automatic transmission, raised seat cushion and a thicker backrest. The polished walnut dash panel with its inlaid cross-banding demonstrates the splendid quality of the H. J. Mulliner cabinet work.*

RIGHT *Princess Margaret visits the home of Rolls-Royce at Crewe. Managing Director George Fenn is on the steps to greet her.*

149

ABOVE LEFT *The side panelling was used to house the rather modest tool kit, which included a window-winder handle in case any of the electrically operated window lifts should fail to work.*

ABOVE *The latest in 1954 technology was included in the radio set installed in the wide offside armrest; it could be hidden from view by a neat chromium plated shutter. A concealed reading lamp was fitted below the ashtray, and to the rear of the armrest was a small glovebox. The rear quarter lights (rear side windows) could be covered by a blind concealed in the panelling.*

LEFT *One side blind is partially drawn, the glass roof section is uncovered, and the rear seat has been wound-up to its maximum height by means of the small centre handle. Seen at about knee-level are the heating and ventilation controls, and those for the division and for the rear blind.*

RIGHT AND CENTRE
As delivered, the car had a full length cabinet in the rear compartment. Later, the lower section was removed for the greater comfort of passengers using the occasional seats. The clock face was then changed from white to black so that it could more easily be read.

BOTTOM *The roof fitments are typical of many of the State cars. They are, from the front: blue police light, bracket for holding early type shield, electric plug for shield illumination, and the circular aperture for the flag standard.*

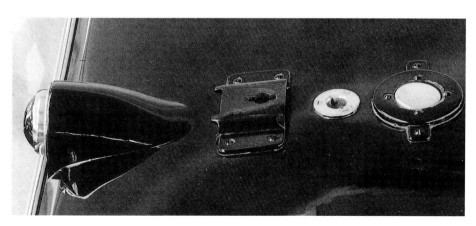

newshounds who were desperate to discover more of the Princess's private life. It had a few scrapes, one of which badly damaged an offside front wing in a collision with a bollard, although it is only fair to point out that Her Royal Highness was not driving at the time . . .

In July 1967 Princess Margaret disposed of chassis 4 B P 7 upon the arrival of her latest official car; the mileage on the 'Baron' being a mere 27,000. On disposal it had been thought best to remove traces of Royal ownership. The roof fitments, police light and apertures for shield and standard were filled in, and the area sprayed over and made good. The number plate which had given so much away to the Press, P M 6450, was changed to 302 H Y P. The car was then put up for sale and was purchased by an Essex Rolls-Royce enthusiast who specialized in V I P transport. Mr A. W. D. Adams obviously knows a good thing when he sees it, for he recounts that without being told the original owner he at once wrote a cheque for the amount required. Now more than 20 years later, it still earns its keep for its fortunate owner and is one of only two Phantom IVs in private hands in Britain.

In May 1960, Princess Margaret was married in great splendour to Anthony Armstrong Jones subsequently created the Earl of Snowdon. As a unique mark of their affection for the Princess, the Society of Motor Manufacturers and Traders ordered a car as a gift for the Princess and her new husband. They chose a Rolls-Royce Silver Cloud I I, which had only been announced six months before at the Earls Court Motor Show. It was to be painted in Masons Black and was fitted out with scarlet upholstery. The chassis allocated for the standard steel saloon was S V B 247. Whilst no doubt the car received special attention coming down the line at Crewe, it was to all intents and purposes a normal production Rolls-Royce. It was delivered to Rolls-Royce's London distribution centre at Lillie Hall on April 22 and just over a week later, on May 2, 1960 – four days before her marriage – the car was presented to Her Royal Highness. The registration number was X L P 920.

This car was still at Kensington Palace in October 1962 when responsibility for it was transferred on the guarantee card to the Treasurer to the Princess. By that time the V8-engined Silver Cloud I I had just six months of the guarantee still to run. The car is now privately owned in Ohio.

Although the long-wheelbase Silver Shadow was introduced to the general motoring public in May 1969, the UK market had to wait until the following year for deliveries to commence. Work on the long-wheelbase version had started almost as soon as the standard Silver Shadow had been launched in October 1965. With the Silver Cloud series, Park Ward had been responsible for the lengthening of the body by four inches. Now the combined talents of H. J. Mulliner and Park Ward set to work on the Silver Shadow monocoque body/chassis. This meant lengthening the wheelbase from 9 ft 11 in to 10 ft 3 in. The experimental department were sanctioned with an order for 10 such chassis.

Among the first VIP customers were Princess Margaret and the Earl of Snowdon. A perspective drawing was despatched to Conduit Street on August 30, 1966, the correspondence dealing with the matter headed A. A. Jones (Anthony Armstrong-Jones). The chassis allocated to the new concept was LRH 2542. It was not fitted with a division. In place of the normal clear rear window a dark 'Shadowlite' glass was fitted which reduced visibility into the car from behind. The rear seat, like the Phantom IV's, moved up and forward, but in this case was electrically activated. Unlike other Silver Shadow rear seats, this one had both inboard and outboard armrests. For rear compartment illumination, two spotlights were fitted above the centre door pillar at either side, and above the rear seat again at either side were swivelling reading lamps. Where in the normal Silver Shadow there were a pair of framed vanity mirrors, in the Princess's car were two bevelled mirrors that had no veneered framing.

Upholstery and trim were non standard. Woodwork was in oiled teak while the garnish rails to the doors were of green leather, the carpet was grey/green colour and the chromium fittings were in a satin finish. As for the exterior, the car anticipated safety demands by the fitment of a duplicated flasher on each front wing (purchased from the Fiat distributors). A recognition point for the eagle-eyed were the opening front quarter lights. The roof was adapted to take a blue light, heraldic shield and a personal standard. The Earl of Snowdon wondered whether a quartz halogen bulb might be more effective in illuminating the police light than the 10 amp

CURRENT INFORMATION

Rolls-Royce Limited are honoured to have supplied a new car to Her Royal Highness Princess Margaret. The car is an 8-cylinder Rolls-Royce Phantom IV with limousine coachwork by H.J. Mulliner & Co. and was delivered to Clarence House on the 16th July.

Considerable attention has been given to the heating and ventilating system of this car. A heater below the rear seat is controlled from either the instrument panel or from the rear seat itself. Heat is also admitted to the rear compartment through grilles fitted with sliding shutters and mounted on each side of the division, as are fresh-air inlets in the form of animostat (aircraft type) ventilators.

The radio controls in the armrest are concealed by a sliding shutter.

All windows are electrically operated and can be raised or lowered from the driving position or by a switch below the window concerned. Sliding shutters which pull forward, are fitted inside the rear quarter windows. A glass roof panel over the rear compartment may be concealed by an electrically operated sliding shutter. The complete rear seat is adjustable fore and aft.

The arrangements for fitting a roof mast is interesting, the mast itself being raised from within the front compartment by opening a trap-door in the roof.

ROLLS-ROYCE LIMITED (MOTOR CAR DIVISION)   BENTLEY MOTORS (1931) LIMITED
CREWE & 14-15 CONDUIT STREET, LONDON, W.1
Telephone: Mayfair 6201   Telegrams: Rolhead, Piccy, London

affair; this was not pursued although the square light fitment did blend in very well with the appearance of the car.

The car was painted in Velvet Green, a colour not generally available, as it had been withdrawn early on in the Silver Cloud III series. Like most owners Princess Margaret requested air conditioning and a stereo tape player to be fitted with the radio set. The car was handed over to the Princess and Lord Snowdon by a representative of Kenning Car Mart on July 19, 1967. It was to remain with the household for four years.

Chassis LRH 2542 averaged about 5,000 miles a year up until its disposal and the Royal couple must have been satisfied with its performance and comfort, for when they came to sell the car they stipulated an exact replica. Princess Margaret had no objection to the car being sold as having belonged to her, and it was quickly traded.

The new car, chassis LRH 10823, was again without a division and had the majority of the facilities transferred from the old car. The rather high rear seat was now fixed, but, to compensate, a false floor was installed which brought the base of the rear compartment up to the lip of the doorframe. The new car was finished off in Regal Red and with a black Everflex roof.

The Shadowlite dark glass for the rear window was now illegal and to replace it a cellular blind, split in to two equal halves, could be pulled down from the roof behind the rear seat backrest and clipped into position. This solution was thought up by a member of the Conduit Street staff who had seen such an idea on the Swiss trains, shielding passengers from the sunshine.

LEFT *The Rolls-Royce press release giving details of the Princess's new Phantom IV (chassis 4 BP 7).*

OVERLEAF *Widely regarded as the most elegant of the Mulliner Phantoms, it is, perhaps, a pity that it was not purchased by the Royal Mews when sold. Did the registration letters 'P M', stand for Princess Margaret? The registration number was not sold with the car.*

In December 1971, chassis L R H 10823 which had progressed through the works to the order of Murray-Brown (the name of a personal secretary to the Princess), was handed over by a representative of H. R. Owen and the number plate 3 G X M was fitted. This car gave Royal service for four years and was replaced by another long-wheelbase Silver Shadow built under the code-name 'Napier'. It referred to H R H's Private Secretary Lord Napier and Ettrick.

This car, chassis L R H 21379, was ordered in March 1975 and again had minor differences from the previous Silver Shadows. Black Nuella hide covered the upholstery and rosewood was chosen for the facia. The rear blind, floor fitments and roof attachment were transferred from the previous car. Plain Sundym glass was installed, along with a Blaupunkt 'Frankfurt' stereo system and the bevelled mirrors retrieved from the old car. The external colour was Cardinal Red instead of Regal Red, picked out with a fine gold coachline. L R H 21379 was handed over on September 5, 1975 and was kept for four years.

Its successor, chassis L R H 36157, was now under the marque name of Silver Wraith I I, and Alec Norman Motors had the honour of supplying it. Again, most of the items were copied or taken from the old model. The upholstery colour and material was changed to green cloth squabs and cushions. This car was also finished in Cardinal Red. Its guarantee became effective on May 21, 1979. However, this car turned out to be very unsatisfactory and the guarantee was called in after less than 12 months.

Kensington Palace made some pungent comments about the Silver Wraith I I and it was replaced by a new car which progressed through Crewe under the name 'Mr. Edgar'. As the majority of fitments in the old car were under a year old they quite happily transferred to chassis L R H 39342, although some items were re-trimmed. Rolls-Royce were asked and were keen to carry out a modification to the piping to the top of the front passenger seat squab. Apparently when the seat was reclined the piping came into contact with the small of the neck and to avoid this the piping was moved further back. 'Mr. Edgar', registered 3 G X M, a number previously held by the Princess, was delivered on February 6, 1980 and has remained with her ever since, giving complete satisfaction – much to R R's relief.

RIGHT *Saying goodbye at London airport as the Queen departs on an overseas tour. Princess Margaret and the Queen Mother travelled together in the Phantom IV.*

BELOW *Now in private hands and without the roof fittings, the Phantom IV is seen here at the R-REC rally 'Rolls-Royce on Wheel and Wing', Duxford, 1979. The event was attended by over 40,000 people.*

INSET *With apologies, the only photograph the Author could discover of Princess Margaret's Silver Cloud II!*

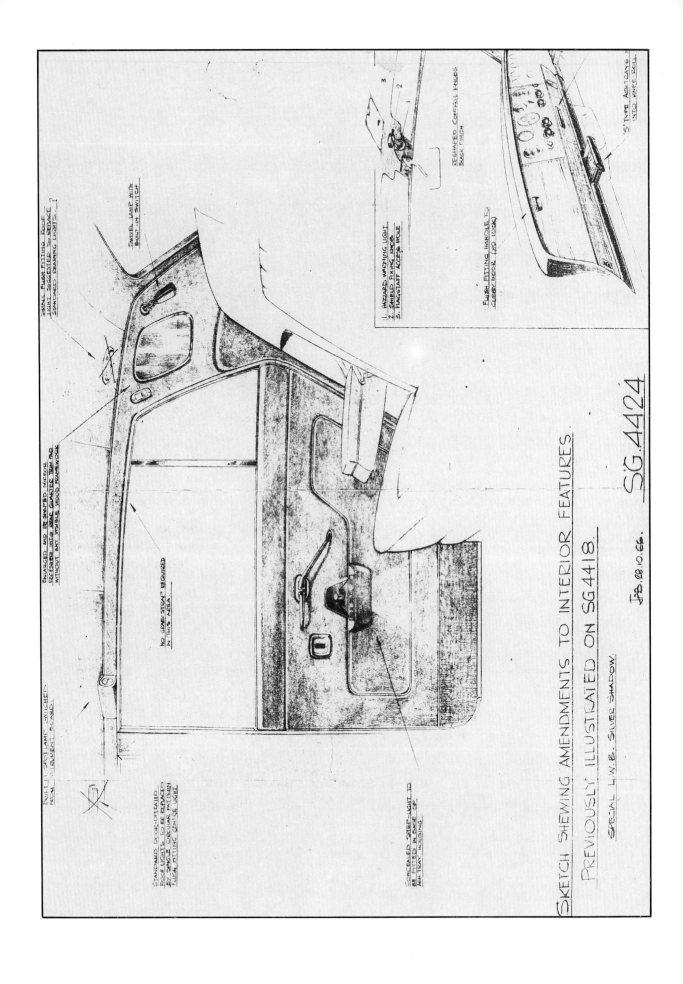

BUILT IN SPOT LAMP SWITCHED
FROM INSTRUMENT BOARD.

ENLARGED AND RE-SHAPED MIRROR
RECESSED INTO REAR QUARTER TRIM PAD
WITHOUT ANY VISIBLE WOOD FRAMEWORK

SMALL FLUSH FITTING ROOF
LIGHT SUGGESTED TO REPLACE
STANDARD READING LIGHTS ?

SWIVEL LAMP WITH
BUILT-IN SWITCH

NO GRAB-STRAP REQUIRED
IN THIS AREA

STANDARD DOOR-OPERATED
ROOF LIGHTS TO BE REPLACED
BY SINGLE CIRCULAR PATTERN
FLUSH FITTING CENTRE LIGHT

CONCEALED STEP-LIGHT TO
BE FITTED IN BASE OF
ASH-TRAY HOUSING

RESHAPED CONTROL KNOBS
BLACK FINISH

1. HAZARD WARNING LIGHT
2. SHIELD FIXING KNOB
3. FLAGSTAFF ACCESS HOLE

FLUSH FITTING HANDLE TO
GLOSSY DOOR (NO LOCK)

'S' TYPE ASHTRAYS ?
INTO KNEE ROLL

SKETCH SHEWING AMENDMENTS TO INTERIOR FEATURES.

PREVIOUSLY ILLUSTRATED ON SG 4418.

SPECIAL L.W.B. SILVER SHADOW.

JFB. 08.10.66.

SG.4424

Works drawings dated October 1966, suggesting various internal fitments for the long-wheelbase Silver Shadow ordered by the Princess. In particular, there were a number of modifications requested for the front compartment.

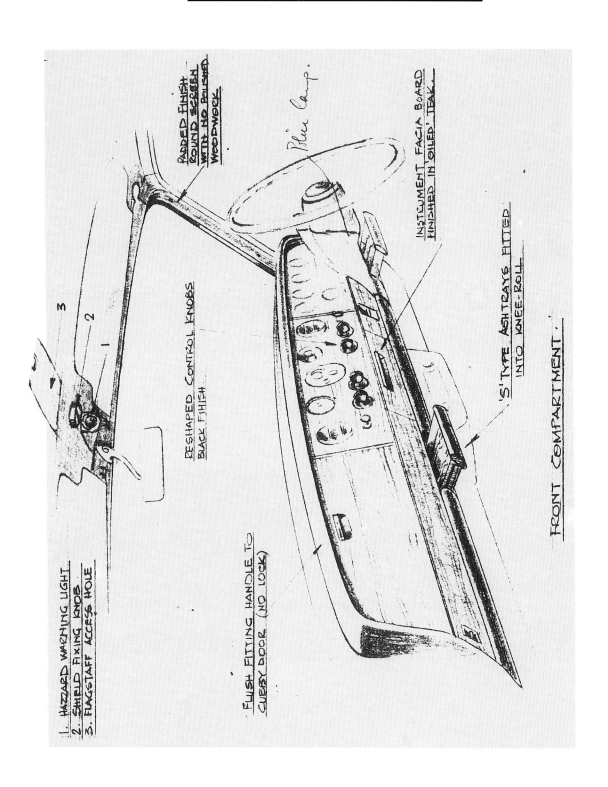

PADDED FINISH ROUND SCREEN WITH NO POLISHED WOODWORK

Blue Lamp.

INSTRUMENT FACIA BOARD FINISHED IN OILED TEAK.

RESHAPED CONTROL KNOBS BLACK FINISH

'S' TYPE ASHTRAYS FITTED INTO KNEE-ROLL

FRONT COMPARTMENT.

FLUSH FITTING HANDLE TO CUBBY DOOR (NO LOCK)

3
2
1

1. HAZZARD WARNING LIGHT
2. SHIELD FIXING KNOB
3. FLAGSTAFF ACCESS HOLE

LEFT The completed car photographed in early June 1967; headrests to the front seats anticipated future developments in the Shadow range, as did the repeater flashers on the front wing – they had to be purchased from Fiat specially for this car! The opening front quarter lights were unique.

BELOW LEFT The roof fitment on the Shadow was particularly neat. Joseph Lucas & Co. Ltd made a special rectangular blue police light to suit the car. It fits so well that it is difficult to distinguish from this view.

RIGHT The Rolls-Royce press release for what was the first long-wheelbase Silver Shadow delivered to a UK customer. It was to be two years before LWB cars became generally available.

Release date : Wednesday 19th July, 1967, at 12.00 hours.

A NEW CAR FOR H.R.H. THE PRINCESS MARGARET
AND THE EARL OF SNOWDON.

A new Rolls-Royce Silver Shadow was delivered to Her Royal Highness the Princess Margaret and the Earl of Snowdon this morning at Kensington Palace.

The car is a standard Silver Shadow Four Door Saloon specially lengthened by four inches which gives increased space to the rear compartment. The coachwork is finished in dark green.

The interior specification and design incorporates many features suggested by Her Royal Highness and Lord Snowdon. The upholstery is of special green leather and pale grey/green carpet covers the floor. The normal walnut veneered door capping rails are replaced by leather the same colour as the upholstery and the facia panel is in oiled teak. Stainless steel and chromium fittings have a satin finish in place of the normal bright work.

For maximum visibility when the car is used on ceremonial occasions, the rear seat is adjustable for height and forward movement and extra night illumination is installed.

The Rolls-Royce Silver Shadow has a 6,230 c.c. eight cylinder engine, fully automatic transmission, power assisted steering, independent suspension and disc brakes on all four wheels. The suspension incorporates an automatic height control which maintains the correct attitude of the car under all normal loads. Its price in the U.K. is £6,971. 1. 11. including tax.

Messrs. Kenning Car Mart Limited supplied this new car.

* * * * * * * * *

ROLLS-ROYCE LIMITED *(MOTOR CAR DIVISION)* · BENTLEY MOTORS (1931) LTD.
14-15 Conduit St. London W.1 *Tel :* Mayfair 6201. *Telegrams :* Rolhead, Piccy, London

KENSINGTON PALACE
W. 8

I hereby certify that ROLLS ROYCE long wheel base Silver Shadow, Chassis Number LRH 21379, has been in the sole ownership of Her Royal Highness The Princess Margaret, Countess of Snowdon, since it was first registered in October, 1975.

Private Secretary
and Comptroller to
The Princess Margaret,
Countess of Snowdon

May, 1979

The ceremonial cars of Princess Margaret don't cover the prodigious mileages that her sister's cars are wont to do. If the Princess accepts an engagement outside London it is normal for her hosts to supply a suitable vehicle and it is simply a matter of forwarding her personal standard to the organizer concerned.

Princess Margaret remains Rolls-Royce's best Royal customer in the United Kingdom.

BELOW *HRH's present Rolls-Royce Silver Shadow (chassis LRH 3942) during a visit in 1988 to the Services Sound and Vision Corporation in Buckinghamshire.*

11

HRH PRINCESS MARY THE PRINCESS ROYAL

Silver Wraiths Chassis numbers W T A 14 and B L W 75

PRINCESS MARY, THE PRINCESS ROYAL, COUNTESS OF Harewood, had the distinction of having the first Rolls-Royce built for the Royal Family after the Second World War. She was allocated chassis W T A 14 and since Rolls-Royce do not use the number 13, her place was one closer to the head of the post-war customer queue than it might appear.

After the War there were quite a number of demands on the Princess, partly because of the absence of the Duke and Duchess of Gloucester in Australia, also because of the death of the Duke of Kent and the retirement from public life of the Duke and Duchess of Windsor. Many of the Royal Family were too youthful to undertake public engagements and so the Princess Royal, who was also a Privy Councillor, found her time fully occupied. In this she was of course assisted by her husband, the Earl of Harewood. The Earl was an early enthusiast of Rolls-Royce, but this did not stop him from patronizing other motor manufacturers, including Buick.

The Princess Royal's order was confirmed through the motor agents Stratstone, who although the main London distributors for Daimler, dealt with many of the cars for the Royal Family. Their Mr R. W. Cracknell confirmed to the coachbuilders Hooper & Co that the Princess Royal would be requiring a limousine on the new Silver Wraith chassis; the date was February 11, 1946, some two months away from the public announcement of the new chassis. At the time of the order the Ministry of Supply still held the licences for the necessary materials with which to build the car. However, these were forthcoming and therefore so were the materials from the various suppliers gradually reorganizing themselves for post-war production. By March 12, Rolls-Royce were promising the coachbuilders that they could probably supply the chassis quite soon.

Although Jack Scott at Conduit Street had promised the chassis for early May, in fact it was to be August 14 before it arrived. The Princess was keen to acquire the car as quickly as possible, but it was to be another four months before the completed car emerged from Hoopers.

The design, number 8056, was only Hooper's third post-war production body and the model was not repeated. The limousine was fitted with an electric division and with an interior heater. The headroom was quite lofty for a post-war car, at 51 in. An electrically-operated blind could be controlled from either the front or rear seat and covered the rear window when activated. There were two recessed companions with reading lamps and in the near side only a mirror, ashtray and a cigarette lighter. There was also a telephone for communicating with the driver. A bracket to carry an illuminated crown painted on a shield was fitted to the front of the roof. The interior was in fawn cloth to the rear and blue leather (with spare cloth covers) to the front. The woodwork chosen was Walnut curl. A mohair rug

OVERLEAF, LEFT *The line drawing submitted by Hooper's Chief Designer, Osmond Rivers, to HRH Princess Mary. (It has been specially redrawn for this book, from a rather murky original print, by motoring artist Harvey Dearden.)*

OVERLEAF, RIGHT *The original specification for the car, compiled after a visit by HRH Princess Royal to the Hooper showrooms in St James, London, during the winter of 1946. In the early post-war period in Britain many things were in very short supply. Even a Princess had to seek official permission to acquire what were then restricted items.*

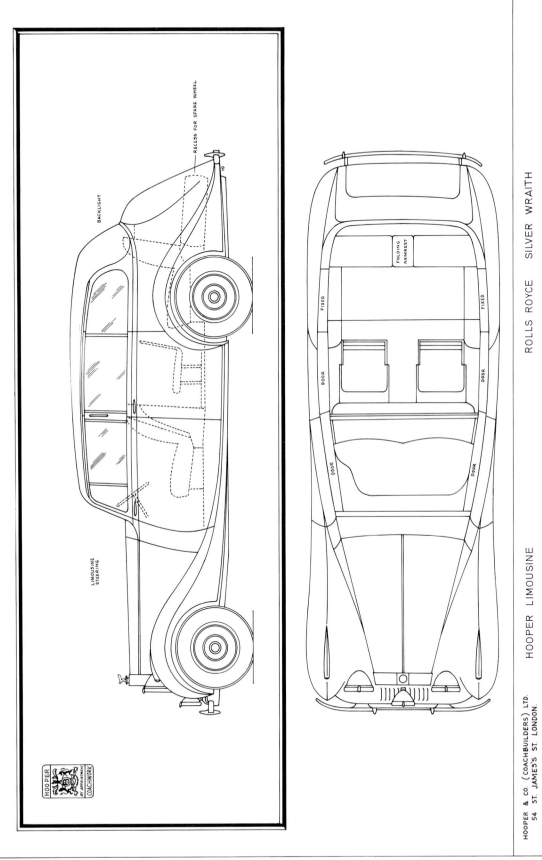

RECESS FOR SPARE WHEEL

BACKLIGHT

FIXED

FOLDING ARMREST

FIXED

DOOR

DOOR

DOOR

DOOR

LIMOUSINE STEERING

HOOPER COACHWORK BY APPOINTMENT

HOOPER & CO. (COACHBUILDERS) LTD.
54 ST. JAMES'S ST. LONDON.

HOOPER LIMOUSINE

ROLLS ROYCE   SILVER WRAITH

H.R.H. PRINCESS ROYAL
LIMOUSINE ON R.R. SILVER WRAITH CHASSIS

Her Royal Highness visit⁴the Showrooms with Colonel
Kavanagh and Mr. Cracknell of Stratstones and the following
details were settled.

Design as 8049 but without the drop line on the elbow
the bottom line of which is to be straighter.

Back light 22" x 7"
Headroom 51".
H.R.H. tried the seating of body 9151 and asked us to give more
room inside, if possible. The rear seat was comfortable and we
should make a template of this for guidance.
Provide a tray behind the back squab approximately 3" deep.
Concealed running boards. We propose to make these wider than
body 9173.
Quarter windows hinged.
Driver is a tall man.
Front seat squab to be made in our standard pre-war semi-bucket
formation with a normal pleated squab.
Ascending handle on the division as on 9151.
Recessed pockets in the lower parts of the rear doors as 9173
Heater to the interior. De-mister to the s creen.
Provide a switch to the interior for operating the back blind
in addition to the one provided for the driver.
Bracket to carry illuminated shield with crown thereon. Fairly
small in size. No flagstaff required.
Own Canary mascot to be fitted to the radiator cap in place of
R.R. mascot.
Deflecting windows to the front
A.A. and R.A.C. badges to be fit
Plain style trimming to the inte
Front seat dark blue leather wi
driver's seat.
Painting - No.2 blue and black
on mouldings.
Heraldic decoration on main doo
Division window electrically op
Dictaphone to be fitted though H.
essential.
Flush companions in the rear qua
Rug rope on the back of the divi
handles.
Hinged luggage flap in boot with
to measure approximately 14" fr
Silk blind to quarter and divis
Rope pulls on either side of re
Colonel Kavanagh was asked to o
the necessary material aithorize

CFR/RGM
6.3.46.

SW1/RA

Tel. No.: Gerrard 8081
Any further communication on this
subject should be addressed to:—Ext2679
THE SECRETARY,
MINISTRY OF SUPPLY,
LONDON, W.C.2.
and the following number quoted.

Ref:-257/Veh/3881/E.

Your Ref.

MINISTRY OF SUPPLY,

THE ADELPHI,

LONDON, W.C.2.

9th March, 1946.

Dear Sirs,

Referring to telephone conversation of 8th March,
1946, this letter may be accepted as the authority to proceed
with the manufacture of:-

1 - Limousine Body for Silver Wraith Rolls Royce chassis
to be produced by June 1946.

Attached herewith are Certificates to cover your
requirements of Hardwood, Softwood, Plywood, Veneer, Steel
and Leather.

With regard to your requirements of Jute and
Cotton, letters of recommendation are being sent to the
respective Controls, who will forward certificates direct to
you.

The letter reference 257/Veh/3881/E. should be
quoted on all correspondence and orders to suppliers of
material and components in connection with above production.

Yours faithfully,

H. J. Willett,
pp H.J.Willett,
Deputy Director/F.V.2.

Messrs. Hooper & Co.,(Coachbuilders)Ltd.,
Western Avenue.
Acton. W.3.

covered the rear floor. For extra privacy; there were blinds to the quarter light windows and the division. The car was finished in the Earl's family colours of dark blue and yellow, although dark blue was used only for the panelling and yellow for the coachline; the front and rear wings were black.

The car was sent by Hoopers to Rolls-Royce for final testing on December 4. However, the coachbuilders received a rude shock when a tester reported that the clearance on the nearside doors was too large – one could place a finger between them. Somewhat miffed, Hoopers responded with 'we prefer not to comment until the car is back here and has been inspected'. They went on, 'you may be assured that it will leave our factory in accordance with our very high standard'.

The Princess at last took delivery of her car on the last day of the year. This was eight months after she had gone into the Hooper showrooms in St James's with the mascot which had adorned all her important cars. This was a gilded canary and had been designed by the man who had devised the mascot for Rolls-Royce, Charles Sykes. It had been presented to the Princess by her husband and for many years was on her Phantom II. Unlike the Rolls-Royce mascot, the gilded canary required frequent polishing and in the Yorkshire rain became dull and spotty unless it received constant attention from the chauffeurs. Just after delivery the Princess's head chauffeur, Mr Parris, conveyed to Hooper that there were one or two things that needed attention: the rear seat squab was too low (this was bolstered up), in top gear the lever fouled the carpet (this was attended to), and a clockwork timepiece was required in the rear compartment.

Years later the Hon. Gerald Lascelles, the younger son of the Princess Royal and himself a motoring enthusiast who has made quite a contribution to the industry, recalled that the Silver Wraith did not go around corners at any great speed and that occasionally, after hitting a bump in the road, a flat tyre would result. He always suspected that this was Rolls-Royce being over-generous in the compliance of the suspension. Be that as it may, chassis WTA 14 served the Princess and her family for nearly 12 years. Sadly, however, just after the car had been delivered, the Earl of Harewood died, after quite a short illness. The Princess Royal was to survive her husband by almost 18 years and during that time maintained the strongest links with his

ABOVE *Silver Wraith, chassis number W T A 14, with bodywork by Hooper, Christmas 1946; the mascot is the famous 'Gilded Canary'.*

OVERLEAF *The Hooper-bodied Silver Wraith, as it appeared when delivered to the Nepalese Ambassador in London in February 1954. It was purchased by H R H The Princess Royal in 1958. In mid-1958, Hoopers made some subtle changes to what had been the Ambassador's car* (Inset). *These included a blind to the rear window, roller blinds to the rear quarter lights, removing the radio to the front compartment, a small tray fitted behind the division, and occasional seats flush together.*

county of Yorkshire at the same time undertaking many other public duties further afield.

Eventually the time came to trade in chassis W T A 14 and to re-equip with a more up-to-date model. Since its introduction in 1947, the Silver Wraith had acquired an increase in horsepower and an automatic gearbox. It was a considerable improvement on the early post-war series.

Nowadays the once Royal 1954 Silver Wraith has a different role in life. In the Leeds area – not far from its former home – it is in use for weddings and funerals.

At this time Hooper had in their showrooms a car that had had little use since its delivery to the Ambassador to Nepal in early 1954. This was chassis BLW 75 a seven-seater limousine of considerable elegance to the Hooper design 8330 that had been ordered by General Shanker Shamsher Jan Bahadur Rana. The car had been painted green with a green cloth interior. It had Sundym glass in all the windows, whitewall tyres, high frequency horns, flag mast and locks to the bonnet. Registered LXW 1, it was handed over to the Nepalese Ambassador on February 17, 1954. The Ambassador must have been recalled because it was sold in late November 1955, to the Hobson family who lived in the Isle of Wight. Their tenure was until June 1958 when it was acquired through Appleyard of Leeds from Hooper for the Princess Royal, her old limousine being taken in part-exchange. Chassis WTA 14, like so many old Royal cars, eventually ended up in the United States, in Massachusetts. BLW 75 as the Princess Royal's car, acquired her number plate FXV 2, taken over from her old Silver Wraith which in turn had been removed from the Earl's pre-war Buick.

BLW 75 was the last Rolls-Royce to be owned by the Princess. Like her previous car, it was maintained locally in Leeds by the old-established Rolls-Royce distributor Rippon Bros Ltd although minor matters were seen to by the motoring staff at her home, Harewood House. Rippon Bros are now part of the Appleyard Group and their Rolls-Royce sales manager was, until his retirement, John Thurland, who in the 1950s was one of the chauffeurs to the Princess Royal. Whilst at Appleyard Rippon, he was still called upon to drive visiting members of the Royal Family when they were in the North east and were without their own car and driver.

On March 28, 1965 the Princess Royal, who had been trimming roses in her beloved garden at her home, suffered a heart attack. She did not recover. With her passing, the panoply that surrounds a direct member of the Royal Family faded from Harewood House. The Rolls-Royce Silver Wraith was no longer needed and was put up for sale. Today it is garaged just a few miles from the home of the Princess at the village of Rothwell, where it is often called into service as a hire car. It is still in its original green, and over the windscreen can be seen the clamp which at one time held the Royal Standard.

The Princess Royal used her 1954 Silver Wraith to visit Inglis Barracks at Mill Hill, in October 1962.

12

HRH THE PRINCE HENRY DUKE OF GLOUCESTER

Phantom IV Chassis number 4 AF 10
Silver Wraith Chassis number ALW 10
Phantom V Chassis number 5 AT 30

MOTORING WAS A CONTINUING INTEREST for Prince Henry. The Duke of Gloucester returned from the Governor Generalship of Australia in 1947, bringing back the three Rolls-Royce cars that had sailed with him. It was claimed that he would not dispose of a car until it had been around the clock at least once; in the case of his Phantom III this may well have been several times. His return from the Antipodes coincided with increased public engagements and his patronage was in demand from a wide variety of associations and organisations. For the Duke and his wife, Princess Alice, the post-war years were to be extremely busy ones. By the late 1940s his ceremonial Rolls-Royces were due for replacement.

It seems likely that the Duke of Edinburgh, who knew of Prince Henry's interest in motoring, mentioned that he and Princess Elizabeth were to take delivery of the first Phantom IV. The order for the Duke of Gloucester's Phantom was actually placed a month before the Duke of Edinburgh's car was delivered to Clarence House. It is reasonable to speculate that Prince Henry must have taken quite an interest in the newly delivered Phantom IV and possibly it gave him some ideas to incorporate in his own car.

Whereas H. J. Mulliner had enjoyed the patronage of the Duke of Edinburgh, Prince Henry turned to Hooper & Co, who had acquired Barker's interests just before the War. They were in fact to body two cars for him, one on the Phantom chassis just ordered and one on a $4\frac{1}{2}$-litre Silver Wraith. The first order, for the Phantom IV, had its chassis delivered to Hooper's coachbuilding premises on Western Avenue on December 19, 1950. Delivery was promised for September the following year.

During the coachwork process the Prince often visited Hoopers to see how chassis 4 AF 10 was progressing. It was on one such visit that he saw the first of what turned out to be the Docker Daimlers. It was a Straight Eight and was to be the star of the 1951 Earls Court Show. This rather grand vehicle had double glazing to the side windows and the chief designer of Hoopers, Osmond Rivers, infected the Duke with his enthusiasm for his creation. Prince Henry, always innovative where cars were concerned, ordered a set for his Phantom. The windows actually gave a lot of trouble over the following years and were exceedingly expensive to replace, which eventually they all had to be.

OVERLEAF, LEFT *A copy of the original blueprint of the Duke of Gloucester's Phantom IV.*

OVERLEAF, RIGHT *Certain somewhat old-fashioned features distinguished this Phantom from the other early post-war Phantoms: twin side-mounted spare wheels, louvres to the door windows, side lamps not set into the wings, and a pair of hand-operated Grebel spotlamps on either side of the scuttle. A little harder to distinguish is the use of an eagle mascot on the radiator cap. Functional rather than flamboyant was the order of the day for the interior of the rear compartment* (Inset). *In particular, the woodwork appears very plain, as does the use of leather for the seating and the door panels; though it looks very durable. The main rear seat had a pneumatic 'springing' system, which from time to time would need to be re-inflated.*

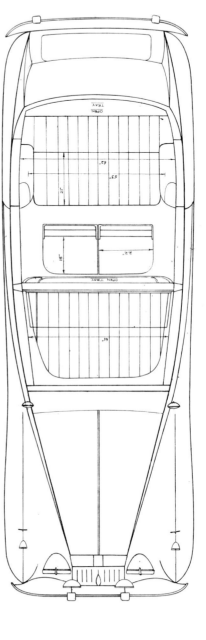

SPECIALLY DESIGNED FOR H.R.H THE DUKE OF GLOUCESTER

No. 8292

HOOPER 7 SEATER LIMOUSINE ON ROLLS ROYCE PHANTOM IV CHASSIS

HOOPER & CO (COACHBUILDERS) LTD.
54 ST JAMES'S ST LONDON.

Design 8292 was a six-light limousine with passenger space for two on the front seat, two on the occasionals and three on the back seat. The rear quarter lights were fitted with sliding glass purdah panels, the main door windows had glass louvres along the top to reduce draught when opened. However, none of the windows could be raised electrically – that was only applied to the division, with a control to front and rear.

In case a rear window cover was required, a flap was fitted which could be folded up over the small window and retained in place with a catch. The front windscreen, surprisingly for the time, could be opened, but when closed could be kept clear with a demister and, on the outside, two-speed wipers and a screenwasher. To enable the boot to be fully utilized for luggage, the spare wheels (there were two) were mounted either side of the bonnet. These had locks, as had the bonnet, mascot, filler cap and of course the doors and luggage compartment. The car was finished externally in shiny black for front and rear wings, everywhere else in matt black.

The interior was furnished in a light shade of fawn for the roof lining and door panelling; brown carpet and the same colour to the leather seats front and rear. The cushions could be inflated via a rubber bladder beneath. The woodwork was solid walnut with no veneers. No companions were fitted but there was a shallow tray at the back of the division and behind the rear seat squab. Cigarette lighters were to be 'the same as on the King's Daimlers' – that is to say, the old-fashioned bull's-eye type. Two roof lamps in the rear corners of the back of the interior could be switched on either from the dashboard or from the rear armrests. The radio was under the control of the chauffeur, with speakers to front and rear. There was a full-width Rolvisor sun-blind at the top of the windscreen. As the headroom was 51 ins a hat cord (net) was fitted in the centre of the roof behind the division. For inclement weather there was an aluminium tube under the front passenger seat which housed an umbrella.

The car's imposing appearance was assisted by the pair of enormous Lucas R100 headlamps. Two foglamps below were wired in such a way that the driver could flash them at the police on the Buckingham Palace gates; there were also two Stephen Grebel spotlamps on either side of the scuttle which could be shone in any direction so as to read road signs, etc. The very

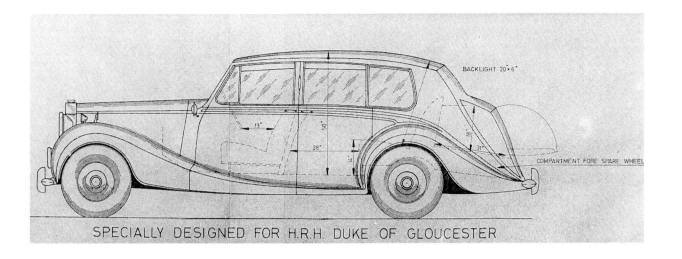

SPECIALLY DESIGNED FOR H.R.H. DUKE OF GLOUCESTER

ABOVE *The Duke of Gloucester's second post-war Rolls-Royce was also a Hooper-bodied car, this time the slightly smaller Silver Wraith. This is the line drawing submitted to the Duke, as the initial design. As can be seen, it shared many features with the Phantom IV. One unusual later modification was the use of sliding windows in the rear doors.*

BELOW *The Silver Wraith just before it was delivered to the Duke's London home. The rise-and-fall windows to the rear doors were rejected; they have already been replaced by sliding windows.*

ABOVE AND RIGHT *These two photographs were taken by the present Duke of Gloucester, outside the family home, Barnwell Manor, Northamptonshire, whilst his father was still alive. The rear view shows the particularly small rear window, and the addition of winkers to better suit modern traffic conditions. The splendid gun-turret mascot can just be made out in the front view.*

LEFT *Mr William Prater, for many years chauffeur to the Dukes of Gloucester, at the wheel of the Silver Wraith.*

comprehensive specification also included a klaxon horn, a fire extinguisher and a St Christopher medallion.

On September 25, 1951 Osmond Rivers (Hooper's chief designer) and a Rolls-Royce driver motored to Stirling to pick up Jack Scott the Rolls-Royce sales director. With the new car they drove on to Farr House at Inverness, the leased summer home of the Duke of Gloucester and his family. Already the number plate had been transferred from his Phantom III, together with his eagle mascot. The registration, XH 8888, was significant, the Prince was Colonel in Chief of the Tenth Hussars. The presence of a Royal car was revealed by the shield fitment to the roof which could be illuminated at night.

Chassis 4 AF 10 averaged about 8,000 miles a year until disposed of on October 21, 1960, by which time it had accumulated 85,000 miles. Two months later, just before Christmas, the car was involved in a spectacular accident near Grantham, whilst the entertainer Shirley Bassey was on board. The car turned over and the plucky singer was later heard to remark that if it hadn't been a Rolls-Royce she doubted that she would have survived. However, the car damage was extensive. In 1966 this Phantom was sold by the car hire firm who had acquired it to an American. He had Hooper carry out a complete rebuild before shipping it to the US in 1967. In 1969, it returned to the UK and is domiciled near Bury.

The next car of Prince Henry's to be replaced was the 1939 Wraith, registered FXR 888. Up to 1951 Rolls-Royce had supplied the Silver Wraith with a wheelbase of 10 ft 7 ins. In 1951 the Company extended the wheelbase by 6 ins and the first eight chassis went to H. J. Mulliner for coachwork. The ninth went to the Duke of Gloucester. So successful was the 11 ft 1 in size that the following year the shorter wheelbase was dropped.

Chassis ALW 10 was delivered to Hooper in November 1951 and was ordered as a touring limousine to Design 8333, and, like the Phantom IV, the body was not repeated. However as the Silver Wraith was in effect the No.2 ceremonial car, it shared a number of features with its bigger brother. The colour scheme was the same, as were the lights, heraldry, and interior fitments, in brown leather and fawn cloth. This time the Duke did not specify double-glazed windows but instead had sliding glass to the rear

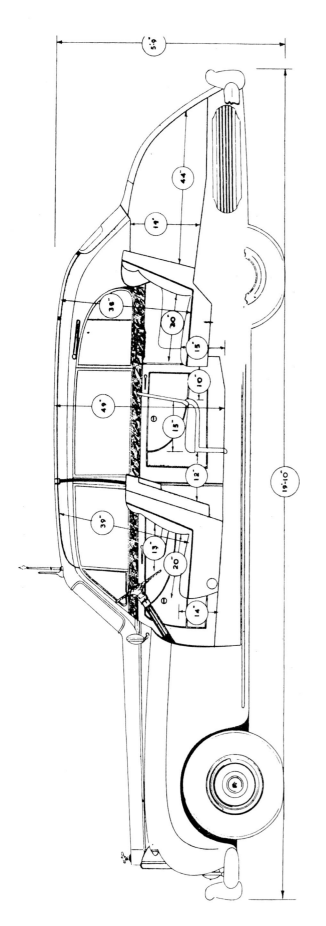

LEFT *The line drawing by A. F. McNeil shows the design approved by the Duke; it incorporated the Duke's own suggestions and amendments.*

OPPOSITE *An unusual photographic angle on Prince Henry's Phantom IV, now in private hands.*

BELOW *The exposed headlamps with their sealed-beam inserts made the Duke's Phantom all but unique and very easily recognizable.*

window frames. Again, the chauffeur had to contend with keys to ignition, bonnet, doors (separate for front and rear), spare wheel and mascot.

Chassis A L W 10 with its Hooper body was off test on September 9 and a month later was delivered to the Duke at his London residence, York House at St James's Palace, the number plates and mascot from the Wraith having been transferred. The latter, in the form of a gun turret, had been fashioned by two petty officers from H M A S *Australia* when he returned in 1935 from a visit to the Dominion. The car went in the late 1960s to a Birmingham undertaker who quite shortly afterwards sold it on the American market.

By early 1960, ideas had formulated in the Duke's mind about the replacement of the Phantom I V. The previous Autumn had seen the introduction of the Phantom V with automatic gearbox, power-steering as standard and air conditioning as an option. These assets, plus the new V8 engine, obviously attracted the Prince and he ordered the new chassis quite early on. With Hooper having ceased coachbuilding at the end of 1959, the Duke turned to the only independent British coachbuilder with experience of large limousines – James Young, who were a part of the Jack Barclay empire. Their designer, A. F. McNeil, had started out in pre-war times with Gurney Nutting, and was to produce some of the most elegant bodies on the Phantom V. The Duke chose a derivative of Design P V15, a seven-passenger limousine. What was to make the appearance of this car all-but unique was the fitment of Lucas P100 headlamps instead of integral ones. In their remaining seven years of operation James Young were to be asked only once more for similar headlamps.

As before, the colour scheme was matt black and shiny black, and the upholstery inside was brown. Electric windows were fitted and the quarter lights could be covered. Once again, a full-width Rolvisor sunvisor was installed and, unusually, there was a separate one for the driver's door. Other lights, apart from the P100s were two spot lamps, a long-range lamp and a foglamp. A radio with an electric aerial was supplied along with a by-now familiar umbrella under the front passenger seat in an aluminium cover. The roof had a bracket for the Prince's heraldic shield.

With the transfer of the A A and R A C badges and the eagle mascot from the old Phantom IV, the new car was delivered to its new owner on September 27, 1960. Chassis 5 AT 30 has remained the No.1 car since that time for the Duke of Gloucester. The car did however suffer a dreadful accident, returning to the Northampton home of the Duke, Barnwell Manor. In 1965, coming back from the funeral of Sir Winston Churchill, the car somersaulted three times and landed upside down. Fortunately, the Duke considered it worthwhile re-building and making good the damage and the car was returned to service.

The present Duke, Prince Richard, still uses the car and has only recently had it re-painted. Its present mileage on official engagements is under 1,000 miles a year, so the car seems likely to grace the London Royal scene for many years to come.

The Silver Wraith and Phantom V seen together in this photograph taken by the present Duke of Gloucester. It is easy to differentiate the polished wings and the matt black of the body of the leading car, the Silver Wraith.

14

HRH PRINCESS MARINA DUCHESS OF KENT

Silver Wraith Chassis number WFC 25
Phantom IV Chassis number 4 AF 12
Phantom V Chassis number 5 VA 23

HRH PRINCESS MARINA the widow of Prince George, Duke of Kent, died on August 27, 1968 at the comparatively young age of 62. She died 26 years almost exactly to the day after her husband had perished in a wartime flying accident on a journey that was taking him across the Atlantic. Prince George was an extremely popular member of the Royal Family and his marriage in November 1934 to Princess Marina of Greece received much public acclamation. He certainly cut a dash and just six months before he married purchased a Bentley $3\frac{1}{2}$ litre with a body by Barker. This sporting Derby-built car had a fitted division and a post-box size aperture for a rear window. Its successor was a $4\frac{1}{4}$ litre Bentley bodied in 1937 by Hooper. Both cars survive and belong to members of the Bentley Drivers' Club.

At the conclusion of hostilities in mid-1945 Princess Marina was still using the two Rolls-Royce cars that her husband had purchased – a 1936 Phantom III, registered CYP 1, and the 1939 Wraith, registered YR 11. With her children still under the age when they could undertake public engagements, it was sensible to reduce the fleet and modernize at the same time, so in the opening months of 1949, the Princess decided to trade in both Rolls-Royces and purchase a Silver Wraith. The chassis, WFC 25 was delivered to H. J. Mulliner on February 7. The basis for the chosen bodywork was a seven-seater limousine to Design 7171.

The coachbuilders had the chassis for eight months and the finished limousine was painted all black. The interior was in fawn West of England cloth to the rear and tan leather to the front. Blinds were fitted to the electric division and the main doors, whilst the quarter lights had shutters which emerged from the rear trim to cover the windows when required. Twin folding seats which faced forward were against the division and the centre cabinet between them housed a folding table, a loudspeaker grille and an outlet for the heater. The rear seat was divided by a central armrest into which was fitted a locker for small articles (a cigarette box and a mirror which could be swivelled either left or right). The armrest could of course be folded up so as to fit in an extra passenger. Set into the figured walnut veneer rear quarters just above the outer armrests was an ashtray and reading light. In the forward portion of the offside armrest was a radio control unit which could be concealed by a folding veneered lid. The nearside was matched by another lid which when raised after opening with a special key revealed a locker for valuables. At the vertical edge of the armrest were the controls for rear window blind, division and interior lights.

The chauffeur had control of the illumination of the heraldic shield on the roof, an extension speaker to the radio and a switch which lit the blue light above the centre of the windscreen. The car was fitted with the new Trico screenwash equipment and there were heaters front and rear. The Duchess always had a St Christopher medallion and this was fitted in the centre of the division. One other interior addition was a magnetic ashtray which the Princess used.

The chassis had been fitted with Ace 'Super Silent' wheel discs and as the Duke had always had an American police siren on his pre-war cars the Duchess decided on this as a replacement for the standard Lucas horns. On the boot-lid were four chromium-plated studs which could support an extra luggage grid. In front of the radiator were two Notek lights with a central light above – unusually positioned – a fire extinguisher, and between the over-riders went three badges, AA, RAC and British Racing Drivers' Club. The sharp eyed would spot the absence of an interior driving mirror.

There was an underfloor aerial for the radio. On October 27, 1949, the completed car, now with the number plates Y R 11, was handed over to the chauffeur to the Duchess. During five years of the Duchess's ownership, chassis W F C25 was serviced regularly at the London service centre of Rolls-Royce, where they discreetly incorporated a number of modifications to maintain better running.

In the autumn of 1953, Rolls-Royce decided to dispose of the car that their Chairman Lord Hives was using, a Phantom I V. (Considering that the Phantom I V range was always thought of as being reserved for heads of state and royalty, the fact that the chairman of Rolls-Royce had one may have been felt a trifle incongruous.) The company decided to invite the Duchess to take over the Phantom I V. The old Silver Wraith was sold to defray costs and it remained in the United Kingdom until being purchased by a Mr David Daniels who in turn passed it to his son-in-law, who in turn sold it to Colin Downing of East London. This last named gentleman recollects the car as being mechanically good (it had in fact received a replacement engine in April 1956) but the interior by that time (1973) was rather shabby.

Phantom I V chassis 4 A F 12 was the sixth out of a sanction of 18 to be built. The chassis had been delivered to Hooper & Co for the fitment of a seven-seater enclosed limousine to Design number 8307. Some may argue that the car was the most elegant of all the bodies that were constructed on the Phantom I V. The Hooper speciality, the rear quarter light window, added panache to the rear quarter of the bodywork and imparted a particular elegance to what was the largest post-war chassis built by Rolls-Royce. The height from roof to floor in the rear was 52 in, whilst the width between the rear armrests was 53 in.

As originally designed for Lord Hives, the car was finished in deep blue with beige leather to front and beige cloth to rear. An electric division was standard, as was a radio which had an extension speaker to the chauffeur's compartment. The car had been with the Rolls-Royce chairman for almost two and a half years, from its delivery in July 1951 to late November 1953. During this time it had carried a Cheshire registration, N T U 176.

By the first week of December the car had returned to the coachbuilders

ABOVE *Looking a little less than pristine, the pre-war Wraith landaulette photographed some time after being sold to a private owner; believed to be somewhere in Manchester.*

RIGHT *The rear compartment of the new Silver Wraith needed occasional seats for the three young children. To the right of the picture is the folding table (in its closed position); below it is the radio speaker, and beneath that is the heater outlet.*

OVERLEAF *One very smart Royal car (chassis WFC 25) ready for delivery; one wonders just how safe the fire extinguisher was from the attentions of passing miscreants . . .*

OVERLEAF, INSET *Very unusually for a Royal car, above the boot was a chromium-plated carrier for extra luggage. Because of the Royal insignia on the roof, the radio aerial was fitted under the car.*

for re-furbishing as the Princess's ceremonial car. The instructions to Hoopers were extensive. The rear compartment was to be re-upholstered in fawn cloth, but retaining the bolster-type trim to both cushions and rear squab. The centre armrest was to be fitted with a swivelling mirror under a lid and alongside a box to hold cigarettes and notepaper. The occasional seats were to be raised at the back some three inches and moved in such a way as to allow more room for main seat occupants. The driver's seat was also be be altered from beige to brown hide.

Hoopers fitted shutters to the rear quarter lights to obscure the interior when required and an improvement was made to the opening of the windows themselves to allow greater passage of fresh air. An electrically-operated rear window blind was added and the original radio set was complemented by a second set for the driver, whilst the one in the rear compartment was moved to the offside rear armrest, above which there was added a discreet reading lamp. A parcel net was fitted to the rear section of the roof and a fold-over type foot rest added. An interior clock (above which was the St Christopher medallion) was moved into position between the occasional seats and fitted to the back of the division.

For evening engagements, strip lighting was installed and the electrical switches to control them and other ancillary equipment was placed in the same position as on the old Silver Wraith. The roof fitments were as previously – the addition of a blue light, behind it a clamp to hold the shield and light source, and, attached to the back of the shield, a location for a standard. Also taken from the older car were the two Notek lamps, badges and the registration number.

Mechanically, there was little to be done apart from an overhaul. The only modification of any note to this car had been during Lord Hives's use, when in early March 1953 an automatic gearbox had been fitted by the experimental department.

The car was handed over to the Duchess's representative on January 30. At the same time Jack Barclay took over the old Silver Wraith; it was sold within a fortnight. Chassis 4 A F 12 was to remain with the Princess for just on a dozen years.

Princess Marina was not a rich woman – her husband's income from the Civil List had actually died with him in 1942. Later in her life, the Duchess with three children to educate and a lifestyle to maintain, was forced to dispose of some of her personal possessions at auction at one of the London art houses. However, the Princess never wavered from her public duty and added a very particular sparkle to the routine of the Royal Family's work, whether at home or overseas and amongst people of many different customs and nationalities. By her untiring efforts she added

Clearly no longer in Royal service, the 1949 Mulliner-bodied Silver Wraith during the 1970s. The car is dressed to take a bride to the church. Gone from the front are the Notek fog lamps, fire extinguisher and badges and the luggage rack from the rear. It does retain the police light above the windscreen, but the flag and shield mountings have disappeared.

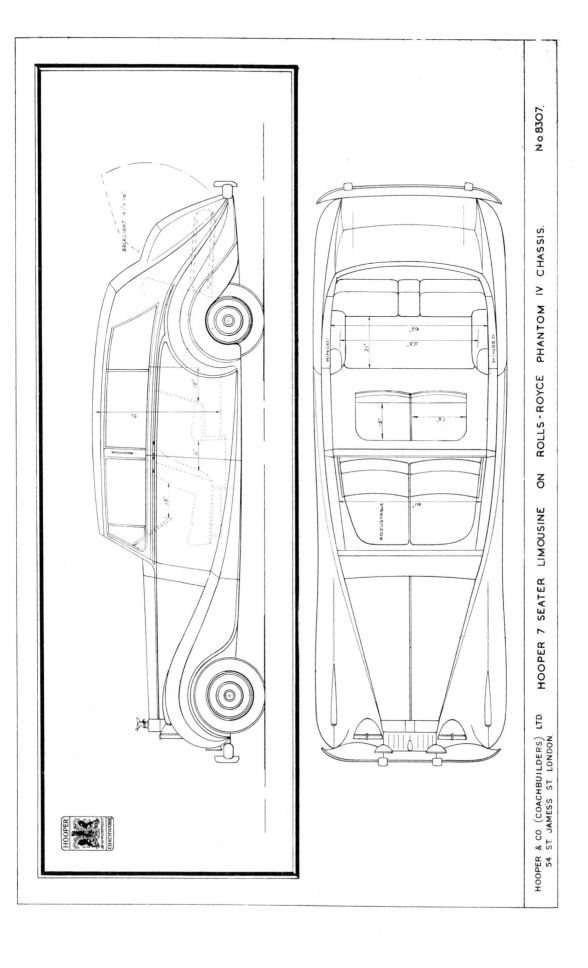

BACKLIGHT 41½ x 10"

HINGED HINGED

62"

53"

21"

22"

5"

19"

ADJUSTABLE

15"

2"

11"

15"

HOOPER & CO (COACHBUILDERS) LTD.   HOOPER 7 SEATER LIMOUSINE ON ROLLS-ROYCE PHANTOM IV CHASSIS.   No 8307.
54 ST JAMES'S ST. LONDON.

LEFT *The line drawing of the coachwork for the only Phantom IV not destined for a Royal owner or a head of state abroad. This was mounted on chassis number 4 AF 12. The body was designed by Osmond Rivers of Hoopers and approved by Lord Hives, whose car it was.*

RIGHT *The spacious rear compartment received some inconspicuous modifications. Concealed strip lighting was fitted above the rear window; a rear quarter light blind could be drawn forward out of the panelling; and a flexible reading lamp was fitted.*

BELOW *At the Hooper coachworks over Christmas of 1953, after the fitment of an automatic gearbox, the driver's seat was enlarged to cover the space where the (righthand) gear-lever had been. Additional switches were fitted to the driver's right for headlamp flasher, police light and shield illumination.*

ABOVE *This photograph, kindly loaned by the present Duke of Kent, shows the Phantom IV during the time it was owned by his Mother, Princess Marina. The Royal Crown is obvious on the roof; and just discernible at the front are the Notek foglamps and the fire extinguisher.*

BELOW *The Phantom IV just before being shipped to its new owner in the USA; most of the distinctive fittings have been removed from the front, including the registration number YR 11. The car was subsequently owned by Zsa Zsa Gabor.*

immeasurably to the popularity of the British Royal Family. It was perhaps because of this that Rolls-Royce, in a spirited gesture, exchanged the refurbished Phantom for the five-year-old Silver Wraith in a straight swop.

Although expensive to maintain, the car must have given every satisfaction as it was the Princess's principal car for so long. However, during 1960 the Princess did acquire a Daimler DK 400. This car, on chassis 92715, was bodied by Hooper to Design 8434 and was used principally for private engagements. On disposal 8 years later it had averaged less than 3,000 miles a year. The DK 400 series, whether coachbuilt or with a standard body, was not a good seller and Hooper must have been delighted to claim a second member of the Royal Family as an owner, after the Queen Mother.

By 1964 the Phantom IV was technologically rather behind the times, and its lack of power steering certainly made the big car rather cumbersome in increasingly congested London streets. It was decided, therefore, to replace the car with a more up-to-date model. Again, Rolls-Royce came forward with a suitable vehicle, another car which had started life as a company vehicle.

Chassis 5 VA 23 was originally destined to be fitted by Park Ward to Colonial specification, with full refrigeration. It was intended for domicile in Malaysia. However, a change of plan saw the chassis revert to home specification with no refrigeration required. The Phantom V was of the Mk II elevation introduced at the 1962 Motor Show, that is to say with twin headlights and improved engine refinements. By now, of course, Rolls-Royce had combined the talents of H. J. Mulliner and Park Ward into one entity, the former firm having been acquired in late 1959. The Phantom V was delivered to the coachbuilders on August 20, 1962, before the new elevation had been unveiled to the Press.

The guarantee card for the seven-passenger black limousine with tan hide to front and Bedford cord to rear, was issued on January 1, 1963. Like most of the Phantom V bodies emanating from the coachbuilders owned by the company, it was to Design 2003 and was fitted with electric division, manual windows, a cocktail cabinet and a radio in the rear armrest. The car was with Sales at Conduit Street until early in 1966 when it was allocated to the Princess.

Mulliner Park Ward, who appear as the sole coachbuilder, had the task of preparing the car for the Duchess's use. They put in dark Shadowlight glass to the rear window, rear blinds to the rear quarters, renewed and bolstered the upholstery according to the Princess's wishes, fitted new lighting to the top of the division and the medallion from her old car. The cocktail cabinet was removed and the space made into a magazine rack with a radio speaker below; a clock was also added. Finally, the number plate from the old car was transferred. Outside, of course, the blue roof light had been added and a plug in the roof would hold the Princess's standard. Chassis 5 V A 23 was handed over on October 14, 1966.

Very sadly, the Duchess of Kent did not have long to enjoy her new car. In the summer of 1968 she became ill and was confined to her suite of rooms at Kensington Palace. She died on August 27, leaving behind an enormous fund of goodwill and three members of her family who do credit to her memory with their immense popularity.

Nowadays the Phantom V the Princess once owned is still in the hands of her son, The Duke of Kent. The only replacement item that one would notice is the removal of the dark shadowlight glass to rear and the fitment of clear glass plus blinds, carried out in 1982. A year previously an engine overhaul costing an enormous amount was put in hand; unfortunately, whilst this was being done the St Christopher medallion was mislaid and was never recovered. In spite of this, the Duke conveyed his appreciation to the company who had carried out the work.

Up to the present 5 V A 23's average mileage is in the region of about 5,000 miles annually. The car, with its distinctive Y R 11 number plate and the badges which had been carried on the present Duke's father's two pre-war Bentleys is still a part of the London Royal scene. Unusually for a Phantom, it sports the kneeling Spirit of Ecstasy.

BOTTOM RIGHT *Viewed from the side, there is little more than the police light above the windscreen to indicate that this Phantom is in Royal ownership.*

RIGHT *Interior modifications to suit the wishes of the Duchess: darkened rear window, quarter light blinds, extra interior illumination, the St Christopher medallion and the seats bolstered to look similar to those of the Phantom IV.*

BELOW *The badges were transferred, but the front-mounted fire extinguisher was no longer a feature.*

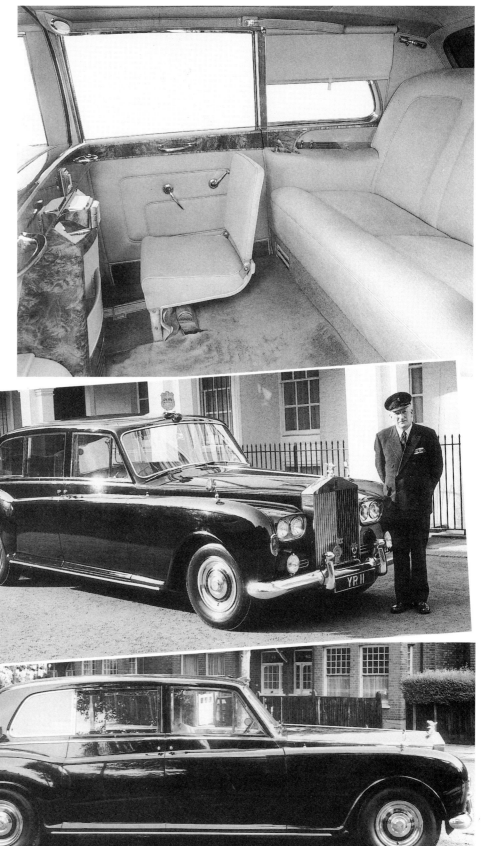

15

HRH PRINCE MICHAEL OF KENT

Phantom VI Chassis number PGH 124

HRH PRINCE MICHAEL OF KENT was born in 1942 and in 1978 married the vivacious Baroness Marie-Christine von Reibnitz. He had long enjoyed the pleasure of fast cars, but like most new husbands he found within a short time that he needed more sedate family transport. And what better than a Phantom VI limousine?

Prince Michael of Kent does not enjoy access to the Civil List and so is one member of the Royal Family who has to work extremely hard both in his work and in his public life. Fortunately he is ably assisted by his Austrian born wife, who, like his mother, sent a refreshing zephyr through the sombre atmosphere of the Royal sanctum.

The Phantom was acquired in 1981. By coincidence, this car, like the Prince's mother's Phantom, started life as a company trials vehicle. By this time, however, the Phantom production line (if it could ever be called that) was making less than a dozen chassis a year. To fit in with the Prince and Princess's special needs, the car, chassis PGH 124, was returned to Mulliner Park Ward for a number of modifications.

The order was made in November 1980 with delivery promised for early the next year. Plain Sundym glass was fitted, with a stainless steel strip to the sills, the car being painted in Oxford blue with a fine gold coachline. The interior was the subject of considerable alteration. An electrically powered adjustable rear seat was installed. In the rear, quarter-light curtains could be pulled over to blind the windows. The upholstery was in

ABOVE *Phantom VI, chassis number PGH 124, whilst it was still the Company's trials car.*

RIGHT *Photographed at Kensington Palace soon after passing into Prince Michael's ownership, the car is now fitted with a radio telephone and some minor updating features such as new-style rear lamp clusters.*

Magnolia hide with a stone-shade carpet. For in-car entertainment a radio-cassette unit was fitted into the nearside rear armrest with a separate radio for the driver. The centre cabinet between the occasional seats was modified to house a telephone handset, a place for about 10 cassette tapes and, at either side of the cabinet, picnic tables were let into the division.

In the rear centre armrest was concealed a small compartment for a notebook, pencils and oddments. The controls for the air-conditioning were installed in the nearside armrest. The driving seat, as always on the Phantom, is adjustable forward and rear within a limited range. The front also has access to a telephone, concealed in the inward armrest on the passenger side. There is a Fiamm Avanti air horn operated by a foot-switch. To deter anyone who had designs on the car mascot, it was wired in such a way that an alarm is set off if it is handled. The roof was altered to accept the blue light and the socket which holds the shield and standard for official occasions. Finally, the car received a badge bar for an RAC emblem – Prince Michael of Kent is president of the Royal Automobile Club.

With the commissioning of PGH 124 in 1981, Prince and Princess Michael of Kent have at the rime of writing the most up-to-date chassised Royal Rolls-Royce, except for the Queen's own 1987 Phantom VI.

Twin interior mirrors (one for the ever present detective), a splendid RAC badge, illuminated crown, and blue police light are all recognition features on this Royal Phantom VI.

16

HRH THE PRINCESS ALEXANDRA OF KENT

Silver Wraith Chassis number FLW 14
Phantom V Chassis number unknown
Phantom VI Chassis number PRH 4662

HRH PRINCESS ALEXANDRA OF KENT is the only daughter of Prince George Duke of Kent and Princess Marina of Greece. She was born the second child to the Royal couple in 1936, and in 1964 married the Hon Angus Ogilvy, the second son to the Earl of Airlie. Until her marriage Princess Alexandra had undertaken her engagements in the Rolls-Royce that her mother had at the time. Alternatively, the Royal Corps of Transport at Regents Park in London could also step in with a limousine if both ladies were on separate engagements.

After her marriage she undertook many engagements in her husband's Jaguar. But following some adverse criticism, the Hon Angus Ogilvy purchased a Rolls-Royce. This was a James Young-bodied Silver Wraith built in 1956 by the coachbuilders as an Earls Court show model. Chassis FLW 14 was a seven-seater limousine to the Design WRM 35s.

All the Rolls-Royces used by Princess Alexandra are registered in her husband's name and he patronized Hooper Motor Services (now returned to their old name Hooper & Co (Coachbuilders) Ltd.) at the time of the Silver Wraith's purchase. The company made some alterations to the fitments of the car whilst it was with them for servicing. Probably the most

surprising addition to the interior was a television set. This was fitted in 1966 and was in addition to a tape recorder and radio.

Chassis FLW 14 remained with the household until October 1968, used for both the Princess's and her husband's major engagements, which meant regular trips into London from Thatched House Lodge in Surrey, the couple's official residence. The Silver Wraith had by then covered nearly 93,000 miles and it was decided to trade it in for a Phantom V which had been built some two years earlier.

This car did not take on A 100, the number plate of the old Silver Wraith but kept its old registration of KLT 995 D. It did, however, receive the plate for the roof which displayed the Royal crown and a blue police light.

This Phantom V's time in service was rather short; it was replaced by a Phantom VI which had been built in December 1971. Chassis PRH 4662 was originally registered JRK 555 K but shortly afterwards it was given the number plate it bears today, JAN 1K. This car covers about 3,000 miles a year. Following the incident in the Mall involving Princess Anne's car, the Phantom VI (like all the other cars of the blood relatives of the Queen undertaking pubic duties) was fitted with a radio telephone in 1974. In March 1979 the Princess's chauffeur Mr Haynes successfully completed the Rolls-Royce School of Instruction course at Hythe Road and in the event was able to bring along chassis PRH 4662 a week before the course began to familiarize himslef with the instruction techniques.

Although the Hon Sir Angus Ogilvy has had use (amongst other cars) of a Jaguar V12 and similar Daimler, the Rolls-Royce, after almost two decades, is still the family's principal official vehicle.

PREVIOUS PAGE *Princess Alexandra owned this James Young-bodied Silver Wraith that was built as the Company's Motor Show model in 1956. Only 14 were built to this design, and 10 of those were left-hand drive. This was the year that the Silver Wraith acquired power steering and twin carburettors. Surprisingly for such a large car, Silver Wraith steering without power assistance was not unduly heavy.*

17

THE ROYAL MEWS

PRESENTLY THERE ARE FIVE principal state cars and all are Rolls-Royces. Until recently there were two Austin Princess limousines with bodies by Vanden Plas. Both these cars were registered, carrying the plates NGN 1 and NGN 2. Both of the Princesses have now been replaced and for the first time in a quarter of a century Daimlers have returned to the Royal Mews. However, as these are not State cars they have number plates, one of which came from one of the old Austin cars. Amongst the cars entirely for private use were until recently two of the old-type $3\frac{1}{2}$-litre Rover saloons, numbers JGY 280 and JGY 280 K. The Queen found these very useful for slipping unobtrusively through London traffic whilst sitting beside the driver, with her private detective in the rear. The number plate JGY 280 was on the first car she owned, a Daimler DB 18 Saloon which was an eighteenth birthday present from her father.

At the Royal Mews, where the majority of cars are housed when the Court is in residence at Buckingham Palace, there can be anything up to 13 chauffeurs in attendance. The present Head Chauffeur is David Griffin who with his deputy normally drives for the Queen; the next most senior taking care of Prince Philip.

Responsibility for motor transport at the Palace rests with the Master of the Horse. The Earl of Westmorland is currently the Master of the Horse and he took over from the very much loved Duke of Beaufort in 1978. The late Duke was Master of the Horse for 42 years, serving three Sovereigns.

The office of Crown Equerry was established in 1854 as deputy to the

Master of the Horse. This appointment was held until 1987 by Lt Col. Sir John Miller who on his retirement after 26 years in the post was honoured with the GCVO. Sir John had held the position for the longest time of any appointee this century. Just before the retirement of Sir John Miller another key figure in the Royal Mews retired, Major W. S. Phelps who, like Sir John, had served in the Welsh Guards. The new Crown Equerry appointed in the autumn of 1987 was Lt Col. Seymour Gilbart Denham who had recently served in The Life Guards. The new Mews Superintendant replacing Major Phelps is Major Albert Smith. Although at one time appointments to driving positions with the Royal Family were filled by the Metropolitan Police, this system lapsed quite early on. Today the Palace receives quite a lot of application letters for positions as chauffeurs. Normally these are filed away until a vacancy occurs, at which time the writer may be called forward. Those with military experience, or work with the police, have an obvious advantage because of the particular responsibilities involved.

The Royal chauffeurs can expect to be on call up to 60 hours a week although of course their actual driving time accounts for far less than this. Their responsibilities include keeping whichever car is allocated to them clean and serviceable. Liberal applications of old-fashioned Autobrite polish keep the cars gleaming.

The older Phantom has special cleaning requirements with its elderly coachwork and more complicated lines. The three Perspex-domed cars have to have their transparent sections treated with a mild detergent, then wiped over with an anti-static solution to remove electrostatically attracted dust.

The open square just behind the entrance to the Royal Mews is where the cars are driven to be parked out of sight behind another entrance,

RIGHT *The five Royal Phantoms currently in use by Her Majesty the Queen. From left to right, front: 1950 Phantom IV, 1978 Phantom VI, 1960 Phantom V Canberra; behind are the 1961 Canberra I and the 1987 Phantom VI.*

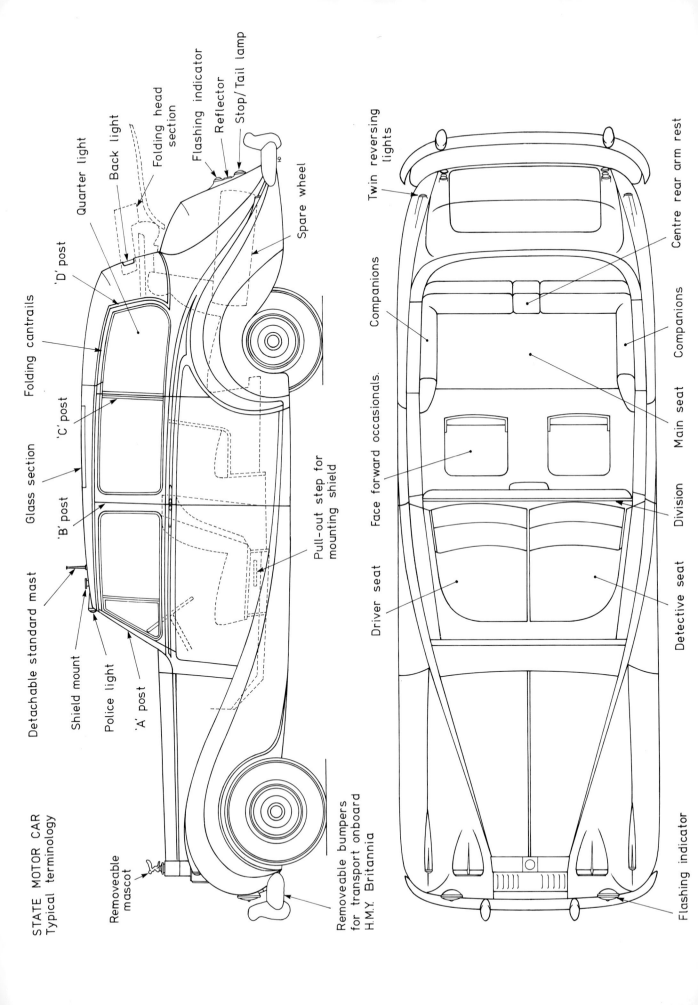

STATE MOTOR CAR
Typical terminology

Removable mascot

Detachable standard mast

Shield mount

Police light

'A' post

Removeable bumpers
for transport onboard
H.M.Y. Britannia

Folding cantrails

Glass section

'B' post

'C' post

'D' post

Quarter light

Back light

Folding head
section

Flashing indicator

Reflector

Stop/Tail lamp

Spare wheel

Pull-out step for
mounting shield

Twin reversing
lights

Companions

Face forward occasionals.

Driver seat

Centre rear arm rest

Companions

Main seat

Division

Detective seat

Flashing indicator

turning left into the garages. There, the present five State cars fit very conveniently, with just enough space for each one. Outside the garage is a covered area which allows the cars to be washed down and then chamois-leathered dry. After this the vehicles can be handed over to a lady cleaner for the interior to be spruced up. This means cleaning the windows, polishing the woodwork and vacuuming the carpets. Meanwhile the chauffeur can check the flood-lighting and the bulbs, the functioning of the shield illumination and check that the Royal standard has not been damaged by constant buffeting from the wind. Normal practice is to leave the heraldic shield in position, although there is a velvet-lined cover should it be required.

From the Royal Mews it is a short drive out into Buckingham Palace Road, a left turn towards the large ornamental wrought-iron gates to either left or right of the Victoria Monument, then across the courtyard under the arch to the inner quadrangle to the Sovereign's entrance, which is under a glass canopy. However, some departures are made via the garden entrance and the car is then driven to the gate in the corner of the Buckingham Palace grounds. It is an anxious moment, guiding the large State cars through the narrow gateway. The Duke of Gloucester's Phantom V is another two inches wider than most which makes it even trickier.

At one time the Royal Standard was only flown when troops lined the streets, but nowadays it is displayed on most occasions. The blue light above the windscreen is only used when a member of the Royal Family is undertaking an evening engagement and is switched off when the passenger has alighted. On arrival, it is usual to switch on the rear compartment illumination in the last few hundred yards of the car's travel and leave it on until the car has discharged its passengers; similarly, the illumination is retained for a short distance on departure.

A guide from Mulliner Park Ward to the details more or less common to all the State cars.

For state processions, it is normal to slip the car into second gear and drive at about 8 mph. Normally, a chauffeur will run over the procession route beforehand.

Even so, events can go awry. Not very long ago a chauffeur requested a route survey but was told that it was not considered necessary as a police car would accompany his vehicle along the entire journey. However what was not passed on was that on nearing Aldershot Camp another police car, belonging to the Royal Military Police, would take over from its civilian counterpart. Accordingly, when the civil police car slowed down and pulled into an alleyway on the outskirts of the camp, the Royal car followed. Watching at the side of the road was the military police car who saw the brake lights on the big Phantom come on and moments later the reversing lights. Slowly the Phantom reversed out past the dustbins and refuse and somewhat sheepishly drew up behind the R M P car.

Overnight stays away from London or the Royal residences mean the cars being held in secure areas by the local police. Overseas, the British Embassy assists in this. Sometimes a local driver helps out for example on a tour of Switzerland an NCO from the Swiss Army was put through his paces by Rolls-Royce International in Lausanne to prepare him for driving Her Majesty on a state visit to his country.

Movement within the United Kingdom is sometimes by train. Going to the North of Scotland for instance, the Royal cars arrive in the dusk at a London terminal and are loaded on to drive-on trucks. But wherever the cars go, their route will have been plotted beforehand and a chauffeur will be in attendance to ensure that the Royal car is fit to meet the Queen.

Compared with the Daimlers they replaced, the Rolls-Royces have covered prodigious mileages. No Daimler was in regular use by the Royal Family for anything like as long as the present cars. (The longest period was about 15 years when George V hung on to his pre-war 57 hps, only changing them in the early 1920s.)

Surprising as it may seem there is no separate ceremonial car for the Heir to the Throne. Until delivery of his Bentley Turbo this meant a heavy demand on the Royal Mews. Prince Charles and his wife have undertaken many engagements in less impressive cars such as their own Ford estate car

H. J. Mulliner-bodied 1950 Royal Phantom IV, outside the State Coach House in the Royal Mews.

BELOW *The internally illuminated heraldic shield was introduced in 1955. Joseph Lucas & Company were responsible for the electrics. Behind the clear plastic moulded cover, the heraldic design is etched on four separate pieces of glass – one for each of the 'Quarters'.*

RIGHT *A feature of the State cars with which every Royal chauffeur must be familiar. The body of the heraldic shield is made up of a steel back section, with a moulded plastic surround to the front. The electrical connections are made via two strips let into the car roof.*

but these undeniably detract from the ceremony of the occasion.

As early as 1905 the Crown Equerry, Major General Henry Ewart, wrote to the Assistant Private Secretary to King Edward VII that '... motor cars are a very costly item in our expenditure'. The passage of time has not reduced the validity of his statement. To keep costs down, the chauffeurs carry out the minor servicing such as oil changes and the like, but even this has its risks. Most service engineers will say that it is during such routine maintenance that an expert would recognize the beginning of a major malady. Rolls-Royce undertake to warrant the Queen's cars in perpetuity. However, larger undertakings such as overhauls, re-paints or the fitting of new carpets and trim, and insurance accident damage, are

The 1960 Phantom V on a visit to the Royal Marines in the early 1970s.

charged. The life-time guarantee does not extend to any of the relatives of Her Majesty.

Coachwork repairs and mechanical overhauls are carried out at the London service station of Rolls-Royce, now in premises at School Road, Willesden since Mulliner Park Ward have moved into the old works area at Hythe Road. Rolls-Royce are reluctant to allow the cars to be maintained further afield because they prefer to carry out the work discreetly and not attract the attention of the Press. Minor work can be seen to at the Royal Mews or at Windsor. Elsewhere, Mann Egerton can help out at Sandringham and in Scotland the Rolls-Royce agents in Perth, Grassicks, are approached for assistance if required.

It can occasionally happen that pressure on the Royal Mews by sections of the media, particularly the tabloid press, can bring about unnecessary change. One recent example was an article which implied that the mascots on the Royal cars were unsafe and if members of the public came into contact with them, they would be injured. The search for an everyday byline in the popular press can force journalists to venture into the realms of fantasy and knocking an institution that rarely departs from the advice 'Never complain, never explain' is a tempting option. If the Palace replied to every piece written about the Royals then a new national newspaper would have to be created to deny or at least explain every story. The 'mascot' story resulted in the modification of every radiator housing on the Royal cars to allow the mascot to fold backwards. This meant that the kneeling mascot had to be dispensed with because the rearward leg of the Spirit of Ecstasy came into contact with the front of the bonnet, preventing it from folding back. Only the standing mascot could be used, and those kneeling ones are now confined to a secure place.

When the Queen was in Spain in 1988, she may well have noticed that the Phantom IV cars ordered by General Franco (all three of them) in 1950 were used for the most important State events. These cars are extremely well looked after, and whilst they have performed a moderate mileage compared with their British counterparts, reflect the high regard which the Spanish Royal Family have for these venerable vehicles. Little is spared in maintaining the fleet and the investment is considered extremely worthwhile. In the introduction to this book, reference was made to the fact that the Royal cars and carriages are the only transport items charged directly to the Privy Purse. Today that is an anachronism. With so much pressure on the expenditure from other State duties the cars suffer from a lack of investment on maintenance. None of the cars has ever had a chassis-off restoration and simple re-wiring is very much an ad hoc event.

Thus it was perhaps fortuitous that during a visit to Crewe in 1987 a wiring fault in 'Canberra II' prevented the Queen's main door window from going up, it had just started to rain and Her Majesty was fortunate to be visiting the place where the chassis of her car started off; whilst H M was touring the works the fault was rectified, in time for her next engagement.

Whatever people may read, the financial advisers to the Monarch keep an exceptionally close eye on expenditure on the State cars. Linoleum is used in the front compartments of the Rolls-Royces; whilst doubtless it is hard-wearing its use is an example of the penny-pinching economies being made, when the situation actually calls for the proper finance for regular major overhauls, if only for the safety of Her Majesty and her family. Every time a Phantom ventures out of the Palace it is on a public duty, going about the Head of State's business. Today, it should be the Government's responsibility to ensure that the Sovereign has the best possible day-to-day maintenance of her vehicles and the money should be found to replace that amount currently set aside by the Palace against a background of so many other pressing demands. To depend upon a system which has been around since Queen Victoria's death is ludicrous and could cause grave future problems.

With the fortieth anniversary fast approaching of the Queen's accession, perhaps some assistance for the running of the State motor-vehicles from Government funds should be given serious consideration. When one considers that Her Majesty and her suite probably travel less than fifty miles a year in the State Carriages, and the superb state in which they are maintained, an effort should be made to duplicate that fine state of affairs with the State cars. If the cars are without doubt 'the best in the world', surely their maintenance in the service of the Sovereign should be equally as good.

Some years ago Her Majesty joked about the fact that the Prince and Princess of Wales had at one time three of her cars out of the Royal Mews. Today such an event is indeed a rarity. Within the last few years an agreement has been reached to make a Bentley available to the Prince of Wales and to the Princess Royal. Such a step has certainly reduced the pressure on the State Rolls-Royce Phantoms and, in a way, associated the Bentley car with the next generation; a course of events that can only be of benefit to the British motor industry and the perpetuators of the products of Rolls-Royce.

PREWAR ROLLS-ROYCE
MOTOR CARS OF
THE BRITISH ROYAL FAMILY

Date	Model	Coachbuilder	Owner	Chassis
1910	Silver Ghost	Barker limousine/Utility	Prince of Wales	1346
1919	Silver Ghost	Barker cabriolet	Prince of Wales	31 P P
1919	Silver Ghost	Barker limousine	Prince of Wales	9 L W
1923	20 hp	Barker cabriolet	Prince of Wales	57 S 6
1923	20 hp	Barker cabriolet	Prince of Wales	G A 14
1924	Silver Ghost	Barker enclosed cabriolet	Prince of Wales	127 A U
1925	20 hp	Barker cabriolet	Princess Arthur	G P K 27
1925	20 hp	Hooper limousine	Princess Mary	G P K 49
1925	Phantom I	Barker saloon	Prince of Wales	55 M C
1926	20 hp	Barker sedanca de ville	Prince of Wales	G Y K 49
1927	20 hp	Park Ward limousine	Princess Victoria	G X L 15
1928	Phantom I	Gurney Nutting saloon	Prince of Wales	14 R F
1929	Phantom II	Hooper enclosed limousine	Princess Mary	84 W J
1929	Phantom II	Gurney Nutting limousine	Prince of Wales	115 W J
1933	20/25 hp	Park Ward enclosed limousine	Princess Victoria	G W X 9
1936	Phantom III	Barker touring limousine	Duke of Kent	3 A Z 43
1937	Phantom III	Barker enclosed limousine	Duke of Gloucester	3 A X 195
1937	25/30 hp	Thrupp & Maberly limousine	Duke of Gloucester	G U N 35
1939	Wraith	Park Ward limousine	Duke of Connaught	W R B 6
1939	Wraith	Thrupp & Maberly limousine	Duke of Gloucester	W M B 62
1939	Wraith	Hooper landaulette	Duke of Kent	W H C 2

*The young Queen steps into the first Royal Phantom IV
in April 1952. This was her first public engagement after
her coronation: and the first official duty for a Rolls-Royce
as a State car.*

POSTWAR ROLLS-ROYCE MOTOR CARS OF THE BRITISH ROYAL FAMILY

Date	Model	Coachbuilder	Owner	Chassis
1946	Silver Wraith	Hooper limousine	Princess Mary (Princess Royal)	W T A 14
1949	Silver Wraith	H. J. Mulliner limousine	Princess Marina	W F C 25
1950	Phantom IV	H. J. Mulliner limousine	Duke of Edinburgh	4 A F 2
1951	Phantom IV	Hooper limousine	Duke of Gloucester	4 A F 10
1951	Phantom IV	Hooper limousine	Princess Marina (1954)	4 A F 12
1952	Silver Wraith	Hooper limousine	Duke of Gloucester	A L W 10
1954	Phantom IV	Hooper landaulette	H M The Queen (1959)	4 B P 5
1954	Phantom IV	H. J. Mulliner limousine	Princess Margaret	4 B P 7
1954	Silver Wraith	Hooper limousine	Princess Mary (Princess Royal) (1958)	B L W 75
1956	Silver Wraith	James Young limousine	Princess Alexandra (1964)	F L W 14
1960	Phantom V	Park Ward limousine	H M The Queen	5 A S 33
1960	Silver Cloud	RR Standard steel saloon	Princess Margaret	S V B 247
1961	Phantom V	Park Ward limousine	H M The Queen	5 A T 34
1961	Phantom V	James Young limousine	Duke of Gloucester	5 A T 30
1962	Phantom V	Park Ward landaulette	H M The Queen Mother	5 C G 37
1963	Phantom V	Park Ward limousine	Princess Marina (1966)	5 V A 23
1965	Phantom V	H. J. Mulliner Park Ward	Princess Alexandra (1968)	not known
1967	Silver Shadow	H. J. Mulliner Park Ward	Princess Margaret	L R H 2542

1971	Silver Shadow	H. J. Mulliner Park Ward	Princess Margaret	LRH 10823
1973	Phantom VI	H. J. Mulliner Park Ward	Princess Alexandra	PRH 4662
1975	Silver Shadow	H. J. Mulliner Park Ward	Princess Margaret	LRH 21379
1978	Phantom VI	H. J. Mulliner Park Ward	HM The Queen	PGH 101
1979	Silver Wraith 2	H. J. Mulliner Park Ward	Princess Margaret	LRH 36157
1980	Silver Wraith 2	H. J. Mulliner Park Ward	Princess Margaret	LRH 39342
1981	Phantom VI	H. J. Mulliner Park Ward	Prince Michael of Kent	PGH 124
1987	Phantom VI	H. J. Mulliner Park Ward	HM The Queen	PMH 10415

The H. J. Mulliner Park Ward body drawing for the
Phantom V.

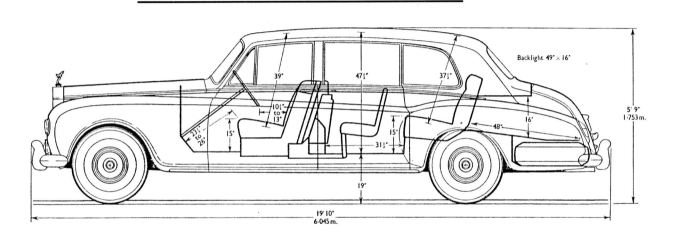

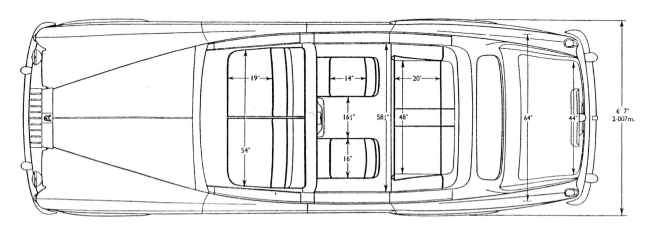